The Exploits of Xenophon

THE
EXPLOITS OF
XENOPHON

BY GEOFFREY HOUSEHOLD

Illustrated by

LEONARD EVERETT FISHER

LINNET BOOKS

HAMDEN · CONNECTICUT

First published 1989 as a Linnet Book,
an imprint of The Shoe String Press, Inc.
Hamden, Connecticut 06514
by arrangement with Random House, Inc.

The paper used in this publication meets the
minimum requirements of American National
Standard for Information Sciences—
Permanence of Paper for Printed
Library Materials, ANSI Z39.48–1987. ♾

Printed in the United States of America

Library of Congress Cataloging–in–Publication Data

Household, Geoffrey, 1900–
The exploits of Xenophon.
Reprint. Originally published: New York : Random
House, 1955.
Includes index.
Summary: When Cyrus and the Greek military
leaders are killed in an attempt to seize the throne
of Persia, Xenophon, a young Greek soldier, is
chosen to lead the troops out of the hostile country.
1. Greece—History—Expedition of Cyrus, 401 B.C.—
Juvenile literature. 2. Iran—History—To 640—
Juvenile literature. 3. Xenophon—Juvenile literature.
4. Cyrus, the Younger, d. 401 B.C.—Juvenile literature.
[1. Greece—History—Expedition of Cyrus, 401 B.C.
2. Iran—History—To 640. 3. Xenophon. 4. Cyrus,
the Younger, d. 401 B.C.] I. Fisher, Leonard Everett.
II. Xenophon. Anabasis. III. Title.
DF231.32.H68   1989   938   89–12396
ISBN 0–208–02224–4 (alk. paper)

Contents

Preface

THIS STORY OF BATTLE AND ADVENTURE WAS first published about the year 371 B.C., but it may seem to you as vivid as if it had been written by a colonel in the last war. This is because Xenophon is describing at first hand what he did, what he suffered and what he saw.

He was born, probably, about 431 B.C. and died about 354 B.C. His chief interests were farming, soldiering and horsemanship, but he had had the most glorious education that the world has ever known: he was schooled in Athens at the time of her greatest splendor, and had Socrates as his teacher. So writing was a natural amusement for his hours of leisure.

He has left us a history of the revolutionary years in Athens; essays on cavalry, the training of youth and economics; his recollections of Socrates; and this great story which is called the *Anabasis*. If you learn Greek, you will probably begin your reading with extracts from it.

It is the very first book of war reminiscences which has come down to us, and it gives a superb picture of a lively Greek army and its impact upon the ancient civilization of the East. Though the adventure was only a heroic retreat, it did show the Greeks that they need not be frightened by the immense spaces of Asia, and that they could march wherever they chose, provided they learned to use cavalry and archers as well as the Persians did.

Xenophon passed on his experience to the Spartan King, Agesilaus, who employed him to raise and train squadrons of regular cavalry for the invasion of Asia Minor. Their new tactics were developed still further by Alexander the Great, who conquered and governed the whole

Persian Empire. So the fact that Greek culture and language spread as far east as India—and, incidentally, that the New Testament was written in Greek—is partly due to the expedition which Xenophon describes and the lessons which he and his fellow-commanders learned on the long march.

I have cut down Xenophon's book to a quarter of its length, and I have given him a more modern style than he really has. Also I have made him speak of himself in the first person as *I,* though he chose to write in the third person—*Xenophon* said this and *Xenophon* did that.

Apart from those changes, I have added nothing at all that he does not say or imply; so you will be reading very nearly what boys and men read in Athens 2,320 years ago.

GEOFFREY HOUSEHOLD

The Exploits of Xenophon

CHAPTER 1

The Camp

Xenophon's story begins in the spring of *401 B.C.*, when he was about twenty-nine years old. The thirty years of war in which Sparta at last defeated Athens were over. All the independent states of Greece—some of them cities, some of them islands, some just groups of country towns—were at peace; but they were poor, uneasy and full of displaced persons, many of whom were experienced soldiers.

All the rest of the civilized world, as it was then known to the Greeks, was united into a single, immense, fabulously wealthy empire. It stretched from Turkey to India, and from the Caspian Sea to Egypt. This empire was governed

3

and organized by the Persians, who were at that time a people of pure European stock, often fair-haired and of great physical beauty. Greeks were always impressed by their height and splendid clothes and courtly manners; but they had no respect at all for the Persian political system.

The Greeks invented government by the vote, and they were very proud of it. Their little states used it in many different ways. In Sparta, for example, the form of government was close to what we now call fascism. In Athens, especially during the war, it was more like socialism. But all the Greeks were of one opinion in despising the peoples of the Persian Empire, who simply obeyed an all-powerful king.

They had no respect for the Persian armies either, which they had soundly defeated when King Darius and King Xerxes invaded Greece. Still, no general had dared to dream of marching into the heart of the Empire. For a little Greek army, however efficient, was bound to be surrounded and starved out by the uncountable hordes of Persian troops.

I am an Athenian, but I cannot say that I was very happy in Athens after the war. Revolution, state trials, party dictatorship—we went through them all. So when one day I got a letter from my friend Proxenus, asking me to join his staff in Asia Minor, I must admit I was tempted.

Proxenus was a citizen of Boeotia who had spent a lot of money on his own education and was determined to win wealth and fame. So he had gone over to Asia, and was living at the court of a Persian prince named Cyrus.

Well, Proxenus wrote to me that he was recruiting troops for a regiment of his own in Cyrus' army, and he asked me to come in with him—not as an officer or enlisted man, but simply as a personal friend. He said that Cyrus had the finest type of Persian character—honorable, generous and very fond of horses and hunting—that he was sure to like me and that I had a very good chance of making my fortune.

Times were hard for a plain country gentleman like myself, and the offer was just what I wanted; but I decided first to ask the advice of my old teacher, Socrates. He was doubtful. He pointed out that Cyrus had favored the Spartans against Athens, and that I should find myself very unpopular if I made a friend of him. He advised me to make a pilgrimage to the temple at Delphi, where I should pray to the god Apollo for guidance.

So there I went, and asked the priestess of Apollo the following question:

"To what gods ought I to pray and sacrifice in order to set out with honor and return in safety?"

I received the answer that I should sacrifice to Zeus the King. This I told to Socrates when I got home to Athens. But he was not pleased with me. He said I had cheated. I had not prayed for divine guidance on whether I should go or not; I had just announced that I was going and asked which of the gods would look after me.

"However, it's done now," he said. "And so long as you pay some attention to what Apollo told you, I think you might as well go."

I made the proper sacrifices and then embarked for Asia with my arms and armor and a few of my favorite horses. And from the port I traveled upcountry to Sardis, where I found Proxenus and Cyrus and the army.

This Cyrus was a son of the Great King; but it was his brother, Artaxerxes, who inherited the empire. Cyrus was pretty lucky that he didn't have his head cut off, for his brother had heard that he was plotting against him. However, thanks to his mother, Cyrus escaped, and was appointed one of the imperial governors of Asia Minor. He made himself very powerful in his own province, and had raised several brigades of first-class Greek infantry. They got good pay and got it regularly, too. So they were quite happy to do Cyrus' fighting for him.

At Sardis we were some seven thousand infantry of the line, of whom Proxenus had raised fifteen hundred. Other Greek contingents, each under its own commander, were coming in; and we heard that Clearchus, a tough Spartan who was under sentence of death in his own country, was marching south with his own picked regiment.

The expeditionary force, so Cyrus told us, was to strike at Tissaphernes, the Governor of

Ionia. That sounded reasonable, for the Great King didn't bother much about wars between his governors so long as he received his taxes—and those Cyrus was very careful to remit. But the fact is we didn't inquire too closely. Cyrus was a very great commander and one of the most charming men I have ever met.

In little things he was delightful. I remember him making us a present of a jar of wine, with the message: "I am sending you this because it's the best stuff I have come across for a long time. It's worth-while giving a party to drink it up."

Or he would send along a dish of roast geese, just saying that he had enjoyed it and hoped we would, too. He even thought of his friends' horses and would tell us, when we were short of fodder, to lead them over to his camp and let them fill up on the royal hay.

In spite of all this kindness, he still managed to keep up the tradition of the court of the Great Kings, where a man learns to command and to obey. He was quite fearless—he still bore the scars he had got from a bear he killed after she had pulled him off his horse. And he dealt so mercilessly with criminals that Persians or Greeks could travel through any of his provinces without a thought of being robbed.

Yes, as a governor he was first-class. He made it his business to see that those of his assistants who were just and honorable would always be better off than those who tried merely to make as much money as they could. The result was that he got the best officers for any job, military or civil.

The whole force marched east from Sardis to Celaenae, where Cyrus had a palace and a zoo. We did 150 miles in seven days, and all the time more detachments of Greeks were coming in. At Celaenae Clearchus, the Spartan, joined us with 1,000 infantry of the line, 800 light troops and 200 Cretan archers who were a godsend later on. Our strength was now 13,000.

Another 200 miles took us to Thymbrion. We were marching too fast for Cyrus to collect the revenues and get his accounts straight, and the soldiers would gather around his tent in the evening and demand their pay. Cyrus was very upset about this, for he was the last man to hold back pay if he had it.

On the march, however, Eppyaxa, the Queen of Cilicia, turned up. She fell in love with Cyrus, and I don't think it was altogether a coincidence that shortly afterward he handed out four months' pay. In return he ordered a review for the Queen.

First of all Cyrus inspected his horde of Persian troops; then he drove in a chariot along the Greek front with the Queen following in her carriage. We were drawn up in line, four men deep. Clearchus was on the left, Menon and his Thessalians were on the right, and Proxenus with the rest of the independent commands was in the center. We were dressed in full battle array—covers off the shields, red shirts, bronze helmets and leg armor.

Then Cyrus sent his aide-de-camp to the Greek generals with the order to advance. The trumpet sounded. The line of upright spears suddenly dropped and surged forward toward the imaginary enemy. It was very like the real thing, so the pace quickened and we shouted and charged our own camp.

The result was startling. The Queen fled in her carriage. All the merchants in the market bolted for their lives, and the whole place was emptied by the time we went off laughing to our tents. Cyrus was delighted. It showed what the effect on the Persians would be when we meant business.

Up to this time it was possible to believe that the expedition was against Tissaphernes. But once we had crossed the Taurus Mountains, it looked as if Cyrus must be leading us against the Great King. So at Tarsus the army mutinied, refusing to go any farther. When Clearchus ordered his own brigade to get moving, they threw stones at him and nearly killed him.

But Clearchus was a man who enjoyed war for its own sake. There was nothing he didn't know about leading Greek troops—except that he was sometimes too brutal and treated his men as if they were small boys and he a schoolmaster with a cane. However, he knew he had gone too far on this occasion, so he just stood quite silent in

Cyrus ordered a review of the troops for the Queen.

It was so realistic that she fled in her carriage.

front of his men with the tears pouring down his face. When he had them thoroughly shaken, he made one of his manly Spartan speeches. He was a soldier without a country, he said; his only home was the army, and if they wouldn't have him for their general he was perfectly prepared to serve in the ranks and go wherever they did.

Cyrus, of course, was desperate and kept on sending for Clearchus. And Clearchus, to impress the troops, kept on refusing to go. But at the same time he sent a secret message to Cyrus telling him that there was no need to worry, that everything was under control.

So Clearchus called a soldiers' meeting and asked them to speak up and give their opinions. Some said that if Cyrus would not lead us back we should attack his camp. Others pointed out— and of course Clearchus had put them up to it— that even if we managed to beat Cyrus' native troops, we should be left without any means of feeding ourselves, unable either to stay where we were or to march away. And then some idiot suggested that Cyrus must give us ships to take us home. Why on earth should he? In the end we

elected delegates to go with Clearchus to ask
Cyrus what he really wanted the army for.

Cyrus put off the delegates with a lot of local
politics. He said that the army ought to do another twelve days' march, as far as the river
Euphrates, and see what happened then. It
wasn't very convincing, but what really won the
delegates over was that Cyrus raised the pay
from one gold piece a month to one and a half.

We marched on, expecting to have to fight for
the Syrian Gates, where an army must pass between the sea and the mountains to enter Syria.
Cyrus brought up his fleet to support us, but
still we made no contact with any enemy. We
hit the Euphrates at Thapsacus. We had now
been on the march five months and had covered
about a thousand miles.

At Thapsacus Cyrus told us at last that his intention was to march on Babylon, turn
Artaxerxes off the throne and make himself
king. The Greek army was furious. After curs-
ing the generals and accusing them of knowing
all along what Cyrus meant to do, the troops demanded more pay and got it. But what really

won us all over was the thought of Cyrus' grati-
tude and the wealth and promotion that would
be ours if we won the kingdom for him. Even the
Euphrates seemed to be in favor of Cyrus. The
people of Thapsacus said that the water had
never been so low, and that the river was bow-

Not a single ostrich was caught by the hunters.

ing like a courtier before a king. So we waded
across and committed ourselves to the adventure.

Now came our first view of the desert—a perfectly flat plain with sweet-scented shrubs all
over it and no trees. We covered 105 miles in
five days, and it was a lot of fun for those who

had horses as I did. The desert was crawling with game—wild asses, ostriches, bustards and gazelles. The wild asses were much faster than our horses, and we could catch them only by hunting them around in circles with relays of riders; they were very good eating and tasted like tender venison. The ostriches completely beat us, and we didn't catch one. But the bustards were easy, for they fly a little way and then settle like partridges, and you can soon tire them out. I liked bustard.

On we went through the heat of August, and down south the country was utterly bare. The few inhabitants quarried grindstones on the river banks, shaped them up and sold them in Babylon for food. Our transport animals began to die of hunger; our supplies of corn ran out; and the troops lived on nothing but meat. Meanwhile, Cyrus made the marches very long and halted only for water and fodder. He was racing to reach Babylon before Artaxerxes could mobilize his whole army.

When we still had some seventy miles to go to reach the city, we found that Artaxerxes' cavalry patrols were out in front of us and burning the crops. From the hoof-marks and horse droppings we put their number at about two thousand. Then deserters began to come in, and these were interrogated by Cyrus' intelligence officers. We learned that Artaxerxes was defending Babylon with three armies, each of 300,000 men. A fourth army was unlikely to arrive in time. Against this force of nearly a million, Cyrus had 100,000 native troops and 13,000 Greeks.*

Thanks to us, however, he was not frightened by the odds. He called a Greek officers' conference and told us, from his own experience, what the battle would be like. He had to admit that he didn't think much of Persian armies. We should find, he said, that they attacked in huge masses with a lot of shouting, but if we stood firm we should see it was all bluff.

"And if we win," he added, "you can go home. But I think most of you will prefer to stay and accept what I can offer."

* The Greeks were vague about numbers too large to be counted. Artaxerxes' whole army might have consisted of 100,000 men, and Cyrus' native troops about 30,000.

One of our officers said that promises in time of danger were cheap, and he only hoped Cyrus would remember them when he had won. That sounded impertinent; but Cyrus, I think, had told him to make some such suggestion. And this was what he replied:

"Gentlemen, the Empire of the Great King stretches to regions where man cannot live, from the cold deserts of the north to the hot deserts of the south. But all the country between is ruled by the governors appointed by my brother. If we win, those governorships will be entrusted to my friends; and I am only afraid that I may not have enough friends for all I can give them. And I will add to the prospects before you the present of a golden crown to every one of the Greeks."

We were quite confident of defeating Artaxerxes, so naturally we were very enthusiastic about all this. After the conference a good many of us went to Cyrus and told him pretty frankly what sort of jobs we would like. We begged him, too, not to go into battle himself but to stay in the rear. For if he were killed, victory would be no use to us. I don't think he would ever have agreed to this, but Clearchus made it quite impossible by asking him whether he thought Artaxerxes would fight at all. Cyrus was offended and replied that of course he would, that no son of Darius would avoid a battle.

The next day we marched nine miles in battle formation, expecting to be engaged at any moment; but Artaxerxes' cavalry screen continued to fall back on the main body. When we came to a dry ditch eighteen feet deep which had been dug to stop us, and saw that the King was not even defending it, we grew careless. We put all our heavy equipment on the transport animals and marched in our usual disorderly columns.

CHAPTER 2

The Battle of Cunaxa

The Greek line of heavy infantry was just as supreme in battle as the armored division is today. It couldn't be beaten unless the enemy got around its flanks or cut it off from its supplies. The four-deep line appeared as a solid mass of shields, with the long spears sticking out in front. The heads and legs which were above and below the shields were protected by crested helmets and leg armor of bronze. And the men themselves were so athletic and so perfectly trained that, in spite of the weight they were carrying, they could charge at a run without losing formation.

It was nearly time for the mid-morning halt on September 3rd when Pategyas, one of Cyrus' Persian staff officers, came galloping at full speed over the plain, shouting in Persian and Greek that Artaxerxes was upon us.

It looked as if we had been caught on the wrong foot, and there was a lot of confusion. However, Cyrus' headquarters managed to get out the orders promptly, and we disentangled ourselves and fell in. We saw Cyrus himself strapping on his breastplate and leaping onto his charger with a sheaf of javelins in his fist.

Clearchus was on the right wing with his flank protected by the Euphrates. Menon was on the left, and Proxenus and the rest of us were in the center. Out in the desert, to the left of the Greeks, was Ariaeus, Cyrus' second-in-command, with the native troops. Cyrus and his 600 royal horse guards were in the center of the whole army. The chests and foreheads of the horses were armored. The troopers carried the short Greek sabers and had armor on body and legs. All wore great helmets except Cyrus, who went into battle bareheaded.

In the afternoon we saw a cloud of dust approaching. First it was white, and then, as it rose in the heat, it formed a dark pall over the plain. Through the haze flashed the spear points and the bronze of armor.

At last the enemy formations could be distinguished. Facing the Greeks was a cavalry division in white breast plates under the command of Tissaphernes. To their right were the wicker shields of light infantry, then the wooden shields of heavy Egyptian infantry, then a mass of more cavalry and archers. The King's army marched in deep columns, each from a different nation of the Empire, and Cyrus was quite wrong about the shouting. They came on in silence, the feet falling softly and evenly in the dust. Pacing in front of all was a line of chariots, with scythes sticking out from the axletrees and the drivers' seats. These were meant to charge the Greeks at a gallop and cut right through them.

King Artaxerxes with his household troops was in the enemy center. Since his line was vastly longer than ours, that put him well out-

The enemy cavalry and infantry columns came on in silence.

Pacing in front of all was a line of chariots.

side Cyrus' left. Cyrus rode over to Clearchus and told him to wheel around and attack the King. But that was all against the drill-book and would have left our flank unprotected. So Clearchus politely answered that he would see everything turned out all right.

While the enemy was coming on in this majestic silence and we were still getting the late arrivals into line, Cyrus was galloping about to make a final appreciation. I rode up to him (for I was one of the few Greeks to have a horse) to see if there were any last-minute orders. He reined in and told me to let everyone know that the army chaplains were very pleased with the appearance of the sacrifices.

As we talked, he heard a murmur of voices running down the Greek line and asked me what it was.

"The watchword being passed along the front," I replied.

"I didn't give any," he said. "What have they chosen?"

"Zeus our Savior, and Victory."

"That will do very well. I like it," he answered and rode off to his own station.

The armies were less than half a mile apart, so the Greeks began to chant the battle hymn and advanced. We were a little too eager, and the line was not straight. Those who were sagging behind started to run. The rest took their pace, and then all charged, yelling the war cry, "Eleleu! Eleleu!" and clashing their spears and shields together to frighten the horses.

It was too much for the natives. Tissaphernes attacked along the river, scattered our light troops without doing any damage and then rode off. But the rest of the enemy on our front broke before they ever came within bowshot. The scythed chariots rushed all over the place, some of them going back through the enemy's lines and some—when the horses bolted—through ours. We opened up and let them through, and only one of our fellows, who was standing still and staring in surprise, was knocked over. But even he wasn't hurt; and in fact we lost only one man, who was hit by an arrow.

Meanwhile, King Artaxerxes in the enemy center began to wheel around to get behind us. Cyrus had been waiting for this and charged the King's horse guards with his own—600 against 6,000. He cut down their colonel with his own hand and chased them off the battle-field. Then Cyrus caught sight of Artaxerxes and rode at the royal bodyguard with no troops but his own personal staff. He wounded his brother in the breast, but himself took a javelin under the eye. The guard killed his companions one after another, and at last pulled out the body of Cyrus from under theirs, and cut off the head and the right hand. Ariaeus and the native troops then fled right through their own camp and didn't stop till they were twelve miles away.

At the time we knew nothing of this, for we had lost touch with the enemy. However, it was not long before we heard that Artaxerxes had passed right around us and plundered our camp. He himself found Tissaphernes there and learned that his left wing had been totally de-feated.

It looked as if the battle would begin all over again, so this time we got our backs to the Euphrates. The King advanced on us just as he had done before, but once more his Persians refused to stand our charge. Artaxerxes was left on a little hilltop with nothing but his cavalry and the royal standard, a spread-winged eagle of gold perched on a lance. We attacked again, but we couldn't catch cavalry. And that was the last we saw of them.

The sun set and we marched back to our camp for supper. But there was no supper. All our wagons of food and wine had been burned and looted. We had had no time for breakfast, either. So it was not a very victorious night.

In the morning we got the news of Cyrus' death. That was a terrible blow. Clearchus at once sent word to Ariaeus that there was no force in the field but ours, and that we were prepared to go through to Babylon and make him king. While we waited for Ariaeus' reply, we set about getting a meal. The transport animals were slaughtered, and we collected the arrows and the wooden shields from the battlefield, and smashed up the chariots. This wood we used to make big fires to boil the meat.

We were still eating when heralds arrived from the enemy—all of them Persians except for a Greek called Phalinus, who had somehow managed to sell himself to Tissaphernes as an expert on heavy infantry tactics. They rode up to our camp and delivered the following ultimatum:

"The Great King has won the victory and slain Cyrus. He orders the Greeks to surrender their arms, to proceed at once to the Gates of the Palace and there to request the King for terms."

Clearchus was in the middle of praying and sacrificing, and refused to be interrupted. He just said that he had never heard of conquerors surrendering their arms and told his fellow-generals to keep the Persians talking.

The oldest of them, Cleanor the Arcadian, said bluntly that we would die first. Proxenus was more subtle.

"If the King demands unconditional surrender," he said, "let him come with his army and see if he can take our weapons away from us. But if he wants us to do him a favor, let's hear what he has to offer in return."

"The King's attitude is this," Phalinus answered. "You are in the heart of the Empire, surrounded by impassable rivers. Now that Cyrus is dead, you cannot start a revolution. And it does not matter how many battles you win. You still will be surrounded by masses of enemies. You cannot get out and you cannot get food."

"That's true, Phalinus," I said. "You have the power and we have the courage. But as long as we have our arms, we can do quite a lot with our courage, and you can do very little with your power."

"One can see you went to school at Athens, young man," Phalinus answered. "All the same you're crazy. I wish courage could help you, but it can't."

Some of the others suggested—rather weakly —that the Greek army might be worth as much to the King as to Cyrus. With our help he could recover Egypt, which had revolted from the Empire.

Just then Clearchus came back, and Phalinus ran over our arguments with him.

"Well, look here, Phalinus," Clearchus said. "You're a Greek. Someday they are going to talk of this at home. They will say that a man called Phalinus was sent to a Greek army to demand unconditional surrender and the generals asked him for advice and he told them this, that and the other. Now, what advice *do* you give us?"

"Frankly," Phalinus replied, "if you have one chance in ten thousand of saving yourselves by battle, don't give up your arms! But you haven't. So my advice is to save yourselves in the only other possible way and surrender."

"All right," said Clearchus. "Then here's our answer. If the King wants our friendship, we shall be a lot more useful to him with our arms than without. And if he wants war, we shall need them."

"The heralds will report your answer," Phalinus replied. "Meanwhile, I am commanded to tell you this. While you remain where you are, there is an armistice. But one step forward or one step back, and it is war. Will you stay still or not?"

"Well," said Clearchus, "I entirely agree with the King."

"But which is it to be?"

Clearchus wasn't going to give anything away.

"Armistice if we stay here. War if we move," he replied.

When the heralds had gone, our messengers came back from Ariaeus. He refused to let us make him king. He said that it was hopeless, that the Persian nobles would never accept him. So that was that.

All the same, the only sensible move was to join forces with him. Clearchus ordered us to march that night and to get moving, instead of turning in, as soon as we heard the bugles sound taps. Clearchus was now in sole command. He wasn't elected, but the other generals saw that he knew his own mind and had more experience than the rest of them.

That scoundrel Ariaeus and his officers swore

a solemn oath to be faithful to us, as we did to them; and we decided to return home together.

Ariaeus advised against going back the way we had come, because we had already exhausted the supplies of food. So we agreed to follow him on a more roundabout route, and in the morning both armies moved southeast into the villages around Babylon. We didn't get much to eat there, for the royal armies had burned even the woodwork of the houses. But we did put the Great King into a panic. He sent us another lot of heralds, and this time there was no talk of surrendering our arms. They asked straight out for an armistice.

Clearchus bluffed.

"Tell the King we have nothing for breakfast and we're going to fight till we get it," he said. "It's no good blathering about an armistice to Greeks who haven't had any breakfast."

The heralds were back in no time—which was proof that the King or somebody in authority was close to us. They told us that the King considered our reply very reasonable and that, if we agreed to an armistice, they had guides with them who would lead us at once to a district where we could buy food.

This was great news, but Clearchus kept the heralds waiting a long time before agreeing, just to frighten them. Then we marched off to our food in battle formation.

The country was appalling—all full of ditches and canals that could not be crossed without bridges. Ahead of us, we knew, was the river Tigris, and behind us the Euphrates. And they couldn't be crossed at all.

Clearchus showed up magnificently, as he always did in an emergency. He had a spear in his left hand and a stick in the other—and if there were any delays in the bridge-building, he would pick out the right man and down would come the stick! Nobody could resent it either, for he himself plunged into the mud with us younger men and lent a hand. What was bothering him was a suspicion that the King had opened the irrigation sluices to show us that in this sort of country we were at his mercy.

The meal was good when we got it—wine and corn and dates. There was also some nasty soft drink that they made by boiling all three. But the dates were wonderful, and they looked like great, golden lumps of amber. The Persians considered that the kind we knew in Greece were fit only for servants. The palm crowns, too, were delicious, but seemed to give one a headache.

We stayed here three days and received a really high-powered embassy from the King, including his brother-in-law and Tissaphernes. Tissaphernes showed himself most friendly.

"My Greek friends," he told us, "I cannot say I am sorry you have got yourselves into this mess. It's a godsend for me, you see. Here I am, your next-door neighbor, governing the Imperial provinces on the frontiers of Greece, and most anxious for your friendship. Now, I have a very good plan for getting you back to your country, and I'm very ready to put it to the King. He owes me a favor. I was the first to tell him that Cyrus was really marching against him, not me. And my troops were the only ones who didn't run away at Cunaxa. Now, all the King wants to know is why in the world you marched against him. Do give me a polite answer to take back to him, and I shall be able to help you."

After we had discussed this offer in private, Clearchus replied for us. He had only to tell the truth: We had never had any intention of marching against the King, and Cyrus kept on giving us different excuses for the expedition. When at last we did find out what Cyrus' plans were, we disapproved; but since we had enlisted in his service, we were ashamed before God and man not to keep faith.

"What we want now," Clearchus said, "is to march straight home. If anyone tries to stop us, we will fight. But anyone who can help us will find us grateful."

Tissaphernes kept us waiting three days for the King's reply. Then he came back and told us that he was going to lead his army home to his own province, and that he had permission from the King to take the Greek army, too. But he would take us only on condition that we behaved as if we were in friendly country and swore not to loot supplies.

Twenty days we waited, and the delay was bad for the morale of the army. None of us trusted Tissaphernes. Still, it seemed pointless that the King and he should take a solemn oath to let us go if they did not mean to. And the more we thought of it, the more we saw it was our only chance. We did not even know the geography of the country, or how many rivers we had to cross. As for Ariaeus, we had no longer any faith in him at all; he was too busy trying to make his peace with the King.

At last Tissaphernes and his army arrived, and we started home with them. On October 5th we all crossed the Tigris by a pontoon bridge made of thirty-seven boats, and in the next two weeks we marched 200 miles up the river. All the time we were suspicious of each other. Tissaphernes could never forget that we were able to defeat and scatter his army whenever we chose. And we, on our part, knew very well that with every day which passed it was becoming easier for him to desert us and leave us to starve.

I myself never liked the truce. There were the Persians marching through their own huge, rich empire, with heaps of provisions and cattle, fine clothes and servants and gold. And camped alongside them, just looking on helplessly at all this, were our own soldiers with little food and no money, yet bound by oath to buy what they needed and not to loot.

Clearchus was far too confident. He thought he had found in Tissaphernes the kind of friend he wanted, who would employ him and his men on all sorts of profitable adventures. This played right into Tissaphernes' hand. He pretended to Clearchus that he was tired of the people who were causing suspicion between them. If all the Greek commanders would come and have dinner with him, he said, he would tell them publicly who the mischief-makers were, and both sides would have a bit of peace.

We were then camped in the angle where the river Zapatas runs into the Tigris—a very nasty place to get out of. Most of us didn't at all like this proposal of sending our commanders into Tissaphernes' camp. But Clearchus insisted, and it was finally agreed that he, Menon, Proxenus and two other generals should go. Twenty of our

battalion commanders and an escort of about
two hundred men would accompany them.

So they went. And the next thing we saw was
that horsemen, in the far-off Persian camp, were
galloping about on some very odd maneuvers.
Then, running for his life across the plain, came
an Arcadian called Nicarchus. He stumbled into
the camp, ripped up and holding his guts in his
hands, and told us, before dying, what had happened.

On arrival at Tissaphernes' tent, the generals
entered and the other officers remained outside. A signal was given. Instantly the generals
were seized and the officers overwhelmed and
murdered. The escort, who were on their way to
the market to buy supplies, were chased and cut
down by the Persian cavalry. That was the galloping which we had seen.

We formed up at once, expecting to be attacked. But the only enemy who appeared was
that crook Ariaeus with 300 horse guards. I
rode out to meet him with some of the others—
for I was very anxious to hear what had happened to Proxenus—but all he told us was a lot of

lies. And then he had the impertinence to deliver the old ultimatum all over again: that we must lay down our arms and surrender unconditionally.

It was a terrible night. There we were, leader-

As the signal was given, the generals were seized.

less, a thousand miles from Greece without even a guide to show us the way. We had no means of crossing the rivers. We had no cavalry. And that meant that even if we won battle after battle, we still could not catch our enemies and destroy them.

Few of us had the heart to eat that evening.

Few of us even took the trouble to light a fire. Many a man could not bear the camp and wandered off to lie alone on the hard, open ground. We lay awake in misery, for none of us expected ever to see again our homeland and our parents, our wives and our children.

CHAPTER 3

Xenophon Takes Action

Tissaphernes knew the Greeks; they were always jealous of one another and ready to put the blame on the other fellow. Clearchus had held them together by sheer force of character. But now that he and his most trusted officers had been assassinated, it was pretty certain that the army would break up into national contingents, each trying to get the best terms for itself.

However, all the Greeks had two things in common. One was their invention of voting and then standing by the result of the vote. The other was their religion. Like us, they believed that the Divine Will demanded honor, truth and courage, and that if a man followed his best in-

stincts and prayed for help, the gods would give it. They believed, too, that the gods were very close and able to give signs through dreams and oracles and the bodies of the animals which were sacrificed to them.

I was as miserable as the rest of them, but I got a little sleep and had a very vivid dream that my father's house was struck by lightning. You could take that either way. It might be a good sign, since I had been shown a great light from Zeus. On the other hand, since the light had blazed all around me, it might mean that I was shut in by troubles and could never escape. Which of them it did mean, we shall see.

Startled and wide awake, I began to ask myself why I was lying there, just waiting to fall into the King's power at dawn and suffer torture and a disgraceful death. What general was going to save me? And which of the Greek cities would appoint him? Here I am, I said to myself, modestly hanging back because I am not any older. But if I don't do something, I shall never *be* any older.

So I got up and called together all Proxenus' officers.

"I can't lie still," I said, "any more than you can. The enemy's plans for our destruction are complete, or he wouldn't have done what he has. And here is this whole army without a single soul thinking out what we can do to stop him."

And then I reminded them that we were fighting on the side of the gods, that our enemies had made false promises right and left, and that we had not broken any of the solemn oaths we had sworn.

"Gentlemen," I added, "we have to fight our way out. There's nothing else to do. And why not fight? We're tougher than the enemy when it comes to bearing cold and heat and hardship, and our hearts are better and braver. And what's more, there are men all over the camp thinking as I do, but not saying it. Let's give them a lead. I'll follow you or take command just as you like. And I'm not offering any excuses for my youth. I'm old enough to take responsibility if no one else will."

All Proxenus' officers told me to go ahead, except for a certain Apollonides, who spoke with a foreign accent. He said that our only chance was an appeal to the King, and he began to complain about the difficulties of fighting.

"You're a wonderful fellow!" I said to him. "You've seen how the King's attitude changes as soon as we show fight. He doesn't talk any more of unconditional surrender! No, he sends us lots of embassies and lots of provisions! But when we try appeasement, what happens? Ask our generals who are dead or wishing to heaven that they could die! Gentlemen, this officer is a disgrace to the Greek name—if he *is* a Greek."

"He isn't a Greek at all," said Agasias the Stymphalian. "Look at his ears! He's got them bored for earrings like a languishing Lydian!"

So we flung him out.

Proxenus' officers went around the lines of the various national contingents. They rounded up the general if he was still alive, or his deputy if he wasn't, and any of the battalion commanders who remained. And at midnight about a hundred of us assembled in the weapon park.

The senior officer of our own group opened the meeting and called on me to repeat what I had said.

The first job was to raise their morale. I told them it was all very well to give an officer more pay and respect than the rest of the soldiers in peacetime, but in war a commander had to show he was one. Discipline was what we wanted, and as soon as we had it we should all feel safe. And I reminded them what the men had looked like when they came into camp and when the guards were posted. Not soldiers at all!

"Appoint new officers at once to replace those who are lost," I said, "and then call the men together and give them a talk! If we can only get them thinking about what they mean to do instead of what's going to happen to them, there'll be a marvelous change."

Cheirisophus at once backed me up. He was a very good fellow, who had come out with Cyrus' fleet and joined us at the Syrian Gates with 700 infantry under his own command. As he was a Spartan, his opinion carried more weight than mine did.

"The only thing I knew about you, Xenophon, before tonight," he said, "was that you were an Athenian. But you have the right spirit and I'd like to see it run right through the army. I congratulate you. Now, look here, friends," he went on in his blunt Spartan way, "we're all wasting time! Go away and choose your new commanders. When you've done it, bring 'em on parade. Meanwhile, I'll get hold of one of the international sergeant-majors and make him rout out the troops."

Cheirisophus got busy while the officers' conference elected generals to take the place of those who had been killed. I was chosen to command Proxenus' contingent.

At first light we changed the guards and assembled the rest of the army for a soldiers' meeting. Then Cheirisophus addressed them.

"Fellow-soldiers," he said, "we're in a mess. We have lost our commanders, and Ariaeus has betrayed us. There's nothing left now but to fight and win. And if we can't win, we'll die. The one thing we must not do is to surrender, or else

—take it from me—you'll suffer the sort of fate you would wish on your worst enemies."

Cleanor reminded them of the story of our retreat and drove home the idea that we could put no trust whatever in Tissaphernes and the King. Then I got up. I had put on my best uniform. I felt that if the gods were going to grant us victory, victory deserved shining armor; and if I were going to my death, I might as well die in style.

I was just getting into my stride and telling them that we had every hope of safety, when somebody gave a lucky sneeze. With one accord we fell on our knees, soldiers and officers, and gave thanks to Zeus the Savior. Then we all swore to offer sacrifice as soon as we reached friendly soil, and we sang a hymn.

After this sign from heaven, I went on with my speech and recalled how our fathers had defeated the Persians at Marathon and Salamis and Plataea.

"And the reward of their courage is our freedom," I said, "the freedom of the cities where you were born and bred. For we Greeks call no man master or king. We bow our heads only to the Gods.

"Do not be afraid because Ariaeus and his native troops have left us. If you feel anxious about having no cavalry, remember that ten thousand horses only equal the ten thousand men on their backs. What's so marvelous about horses? Did you ever see anyone die in battle from the bite or kick of a horse? Cavalry? We're a lot better mounted on our own stout legs! What's cavalry? A lot of men hanging onto their horses' necks, just as frightened of falling off as they are of us!* A cavalryman has only one advantage—it's a lot easier for him to run away.

"Now, what about food? Well, which would you rather do? Buy it in Tissaphernes' market when you know the prices are outrageous and all of us are broke? Or march out and take it?

"Rivers—how are we going to cross the rivers? March up 'em to the source, of course! But suppose we can't? Well, what about all the tribes who are in open revolt against the King?

* The Greeks and Persians rode without stirrups.

They seem to be getting along very nicely in the territory they hold. If the worst comes to the worst, we can do the same and settle down.

"Still, I suppose you *do* want to go home, and the question before us is how to make the long march in safety. I put it to the meeting that we must travel light. We must burn our wagons, burn our tents and get rid of everything except what we need to cook, eat and fight, so that no one is carrying baggage when he ought to be carrying arms. And if we find we are short of any essentials, we'll take them from the enemy.

"My second proposal is that the army should voluntarily submit to severe discipline. You remember Clearchus. I want to see not one Clearchus but ten thousand. I ask you to vote that each man must back up his officers in enforcing punishment for the slightest disobedience."

Every soldier put up his hand, and my two motions were carried.

Then I put to them the question of tactics, and proposed that we should march in hollow square with the heavy infantry enclosing the animals. I suggested that Cheirisophus, as a Spartan, ought to command the main body, and that the two senior generals should be responsible for the flanks. The rear guard, which was going to have to march and fight at the same time, should be commanded by the two youngest of us, Timasion and myself.

Straightway we burned the tents and wagons and divided up whatever remained so that nobody was short of any essential article of equipment. Then we declared formal war on the whole Persian Empire and marched.

We crossed the river Zapatas without much difficulty, and then the Persians attacked the rear of the column with some two hundred cavalry and four hundred slingers and archers. We suffered a lot of casualties, and our Cretan archers, who were with the main body, couldn't get within range of the enemy.

Under this punishment there was nothing to do but attack, and that I did. But the Persians were lightly armed and far too quick on their feet; we couldn't catch one of them. Nor could we chase them very far, for fear of being sepa-

A Persian soldier

rated from the main body. Meanwhile, the Persian cavalry, shooting backward from the saddle even when they were running away, did a lot of damage. I wished that what I had said about cavalry to cheer up the troops had been true.

In the whole day we covered only two and a half miles, and I got a tongue-lashing from Cheirisophus and the generals. They rather implied that Athenians were grand at making speeches but didn't know the first thing about rear-guard actions. I had to admit that we had taken a lot of exercise for no purpose, but my excuse was that I couldn't let the men be shot up as if they were targets on the range. And I pointed out the lesson—that we must have slingers and cavalry.

I knew there were some men in the army from the Island of Rhodes, and that the Rhodian sling had twice the range of the Persian. That was because the Rhodians fired lead shot, while the Persians used stones as big as your fist. So I persuaded my fellow-generals to call for volunteers and to pay for any slings that existed and any more that could be made.

I also got leave to raise a skeleton force of cavalry. These I mounted on my own horses, some that had belonged to Clearchus and some that we had captured from the enemy and were using as pack animals. That very night we enrolled a force of 200 slingers and fifty men who could ride. We fixed up this little squadron with leather jackets and breastplates, and gave the command to Lycius, a fellow-countryman of mine.

A smart little rear-guard action the next day gave them confidence. The Persians tried the same old trick of shoot-and-run, but as soon as we came under heavy fire the new squadron charged them. And although they had a thousand horse against us, we caught them with their backs to a stream and took eighteen prisoners. We also got in among their infantry, and when we had finished with them the corpses didn't look at all pretty.

Soon afterward the road led us back to the banks of the Tigris, and we came to a huge ruined city called Larissa. Here we saw a stone pyramid 200 feet high on which a whole crowd of villagers from round about had taken refuge. Eighteen miles farther on we found another city—a colossal, deserted fortress surrounded by a wall of polished stones with shells in them, and a high brick wall on top of that.*

The next day Tissaphernes caught up with us, heading a really powerful force—his own army, the native troops who had belonged to Cyrus and reinforcements from the King. He surrounded our rear and flanks with clouds of cavalry and archers but did not dare to attack at close quarters. We could retaliate now with our own archers and the new Rhodian slingers. The masses of the enemy were so great that they simply could not miss. Tissaphernes promptly retired out of range, and we picked up the Persian arrows. Our Cretans found them very useful for practicing high trajectory shooting.

On we went for another week, with the rear guard and flanks in action all the time. But we had plenty of food, for the villages in the plain of the Tigris were well stocked with grain. We changed our hollow-square formation, for we found that it disordered the whole army when-

*Both these ruins were parts of Nineveh.

ever we had to march through a narrow defile. Instead we used a system of echelons—companies which fell back from the column whenever it was crowded together, and doubled up into position again as soon as the obstacle had been passed.

We came to the first foothills of the mountains on November 3rd, and thanked Heaven that at last we were in country where we could not be annoyed by the enemy cavalry. However, we had our first taste of mountain warfare, and it was worse. The army was caught in a valley, and the enemy poured arrows and sling-stones into us from both slopes. I saw the Persian officers flogging their men into battle.

Our own slingers and archers were shot to pieces and huddled together with the transport under cover of the infantry of the line. Attacks up the hillsides drove off the enemy, but on coming down again to join the main body, our men had to expose their backs and suffered badly. We freed ourselves at last by throwing out a flank guard of light infantry which marched across country, up- and downhill, parallel to the road.

After that we had a stroke of luck, for we dropped right into a big depot of wine and rations which had been collected by the provincial governor. So we halted for three days and called for volunteers who knew something about doctoring, as we had a lot of wounded. Eight army surgeons were appointed.

While we were camped on our own ground we never had any trouble from the enemy. But as soon as we moved, they swarmed onto the tail of the column and we had to march and fight at the same time. So we tried to slip away from them in the night. This wasn't difficult because they always camped at least six miles away from us. A Persian army is useless at night, for the soldiers hobble their horses and thus have to catch and saddle them before they can take any action.

But breaking contact with the enemy did not pay. They got ahead of us and occupied a hill beneath which we had to pass.

When Cheirisophus saw that this strong point had to be taken by assault at all costs, he sent an order down the column that I was to come up at once with all the light infantry from the rear guard. I couldn't do this, for I was in touch with Tissaphernes and his whole force. So I galloped up to the front and explained to him what the position was.

"And what about mine?" he said. "Look at those fellows up there!"

He was right. They had to be dislodged. Fortunately there was a peak rising straight above the road, and from it a possible path led to the shoulder where the enemy were. If we could occupy the peak before they did, we could easily turn them out of their position.

"Let's make a dash for it, Cheirisophus," I suggested. "Take command of the party yourself, and I'll stay here. Or, if you think it wiser, you stay and I'll go."

"You can do which you please," said Cheirisophus, who was still a bit annoyed because I had used my common sense about the rear guard.

As I was the younger, I chose the climb; and Cheirisophus gave me the light infantry from the vanguard and his own company of 300 hand-picked toughs.

When the enemy spotted what we were up

Parties from the two armies made a dash for the peak.

Both the Greeks and Persians cheered their men on.

to, they, too, made a dash for the peak. It was like a race in full view of both armies, and the noise from the stands was terrific—Greeks and Persians each cheering their own men on.

I was still mounted, and rode along the ranks shouting that the sooner they got up the hill, the sooner they'd get back to their wives and children, and all that sort of thing.

"Play fair, Xenophon!" said a man from Sicyon called Soteridas. "You're sitting on your fat horse, and I'm carrying a shield!"

Only one reply to that! I jumped off my horse, shoved Soteridas out of the line and took his shield. It nearly finished me, for I was wearing my heavy cavalry breastplate as well and using all my breath to cheer the men on. However, the rest of them chucked stones at Soteridas and told him to take his shield back and get going. So I remounted, rode as far as my horse could go and did the rest of the climb on foot. We reached the top first, and the natives broke and fled.

CHAPTER 4

Kurdestan

The Greeks were now north of Mosul, near the present frontier between Iraq and Turkey. They had no maps, and the country ahead of them was utterly unknown and inhabited by wild, unconquerable mountain tribes.

In the world of that time no people but the Greeks would ever have attempted such a march. They alone had the discipline—and the intelligence. Their quick minds could learn by experience. Xenophon and his fellow-generals had imitated the Persian cavalry charge. And they were beginning to use light infantry, which had never had any importance in Greece, just as a modern commander would. The lessons *they learned made it possible, seventy years later, for Alexander to conquer the whole Middle East and to change human history.*

When Cheirisophus and the main body of the army had come down from the hills, they found themselves again in the valley of the Tigris. Parties at once set off to lift cattle and supplies from the nearby villages, and were cut up by the Persian cavalry. Tissaphernes promptly set fire to the villages, so all their hopes of a decent meal were disappointed.

Cheirisophus had to march out in force to rescue his men, and I met his column as my mountain party and I were making our way down to the plain. They were pretty downhearted and I did my best to cheer them up.

"If Tissaphernes is burning the villages," I said, "it looks to me as if he has at last admitted that the country is ours, and not the King's. What do you think, Cheirisophus? Shall we fight for it?"

"No," he answered. "There's a better trick than that. We'll burn some villages ourselves.

That'll puzzle 'em! They'll begin to wonder if we mean to starve them, too."

In this country we seemed to have come to a dead end. We had either to cross the Tigris or march into unknown mountains or go back. We looked at the Tigris and sounded its depth with our spears. It couldn't be crossed. One of our Rhodian soldiers had an ingenious idea of making a bridge of skins blown up into balloons. This might have worked, but all the Persian cavalry were in position on the opposite bank to stop us landing. So we decided to go back, but, before we did, we carried out Cheirisophus' suggestion of burning all the villages in sight.

This bluff completely beat Tissaphernes and Ariaeus, who could not make out what our next move would be. When they saw that we had turned back toward Babylon, they continued their march to the west. We never set eyes on them again.

What to do next we did not know, so the generals had all the prisoners brought up to headquarters to be questioned on the geography. We learned that if we marched east we should come to the highlands of Persia and the capitals of Ecbatana and Susa, where the Great King used to spend the summer. That was of no more use to us than the road south to Babylon.

The road to the west led to Asia Minor. But that was the route Tissaphernes had taken, and we had had quite enough of him. So the only possibility left was to march north into the country of the Kurds.

The prisoners told us that these Kurds were a very warlike people who had destroyed to the last man an army of 120,000 men which the King had sent against them. But if, they said, we could force our way through the mountains of Kurdestan, we should come to Armenia. This was a rich and prosperous province of the Empire with roads leading anywhere we might want to go.

The first of the mountain passes was close to us. We decided that it must be captured at once before the Kurds could defend it. So we told the men to turn in as they were and be ready to march after midnight.

After prayers and sacrifices, we crossed the

plain under cover of darkness. At dawn we were in the pass. Cheirisophus led the advance with all our light infantry, and I took the rear guard as usual. Since there seemed to be no more danger of attacks on the tail of the column, I had only the heavy infantry of the line.

In the valleys and on the terraces of the mountains were lots of tiny villages. They were all deserted, for the Kurds with their women and children had fled to the high ground. We took what food we needed and were careful not to loot—though they had some fine bronze pots and pans—for we still hoped that the Kurds might let us through in peace. We called to them whenever we saw them, telling them that we, too, were enemies of the Great King, but they made no reply.

We were on the march for some sixteen hours, and it was dark again when we came out into kinder country. Just as my rear guard were emerging from the pass, we were smartly attacked by a small body of Kurds who surprised us and did a lot of damage. This was a nasty warning. If they had had time to concentrate a larger force, they could have wiped out half our army in the dark. We bivouacked in the valley, and we didn't like it. All around us, in a circle on the mountains, were the watch fires of the Kurds.

The next morning, which was November 13th, the generals determined to abandon all prisoners, slaves and noncombatants, all unnecessary private property, and any of the transport animals that were weak. To see that our order was obeyed we posted ourselves at the narrowest part of the road and confiscated anything we didn't approve of.

That day passed with only a little fighting, but on the next a great mountain storm swept over us. We could not camp because we were again short of food. With the storm came the Kurdish arrows, so we were continually trying to clear the pass and making mighty little progress. Again and again I would send a runner up to the head of the column, asking Cheirisophus to slow down. Usually he did, but once or twice he just told us to stop our counterattacks and hurry up. The march, at any rate in the rear guard, became uncommonly like a run. I lost

A Kurdish archer

two first-class men here—a Spartan shot through shield and leather jacket and an Arcadian shot clean through the helmet.

I've never seen anything like those Kurdish archers. Their bows were five feet long, and they drew the string with the left foot planted against the lower end of the bow. The arrows were a yard long and so heavy that we picked them up, fitted them to our throwing thongs and used them as javelins.

When at last we came into camp, I had it out with Cheirisophus. But as usual he was right.

"Look at that path going straight up the mountain!" he said. "And remember we have to follow it! That's why I was in a hurry—to seize the pass before the Kurds could get there first. Well, they have—as you can see by that mass of men up there. The guides say there is no other way."

The position was desperate. I had a couple of Kurdish prisoners whom we had taken in a counterattack, and I suggested to Cheirisophus that we should question them separately. The first denied and kept on denying that there was any other path, in spite of all we did to him. That one was killed, and when the other Kurd saw what had happened to him, he talked.

"There is a way around," he told us, "and good enough for pack animals. My friend, he wouldn't speak about it because he has a married daughter who lives along the road. But I will take you."

We asked what difficulties we had to expect, and found out from him that there was a ridge which we must seize and hold if the army was to have any hope of getting through. So we called an officers' conference, explained the situation and asked for volunteers.

Three Arcadian officers of the line stepped forward, as did a light-infantry captain who had a fine record of gallantry. They collected an assault party of 2,000 men, had a quick bite to eat and set off at once with the prisoner as guide. The dusk was coming down and torrents of rain with it.

The rear guard under my command marched straight for the high pass which the enemy were holding in force. It was only a feigned attack to distract their attention, but we couldn't have driven it home even if we had wished. The Kurds began to roll down boulders, some of them weighing tons, which smashed and splintered on the rocks around us. It was just like being under heavy fire from slings. We kept on probing their position until it was dark, and then returned to camp. All night long the enemy went on rolling their great stones, and we could hear them booming and crashing in the ravine.

Meanwhile, the assault party surprised a strong enemy post near the top of the ridge. They assumed then that their job was done. In the morning they found it wasn't, for they had captured merely an outpost. But fortunately dawn broke with a mist, and they were able to creep up on the Kurds who were holding the main mountain pass. They sounded their trumpets as a signal to us, who were waiting far below them, that they were going into action. Then they charged and swept the enemy off the mountain.

At the call of the trumpets Cheirisophus

The Kurds began to roll down great boulders on the pass.

attacked straight up the road, and the other generals led their contingents at the steep hillsides, the men hauling each other up with their spears. I, with the rear guard and all the transport animals, followed the side road over the ridge. The assault party had cleared it and gone on, but now the enemy had had time to reform. We had to storm three separate crests to get through. Coming down the last of them, I had a narrow escape. The enemy were hot on our tail; they rolled down rocks again, uttering terrific yells. My orderly, who was carrying my shield, bolted. I was saved only because Eurylochus, an Arcadian, ran up and covered the pair of us with his shield.

The end of the day, with all the army reunited, was thoroughly satisfactory. We found ourselves in a district of really well-built houses, with plenty of provisions in the barns and big cemented cisterns full of wine. Cheirisophus and I arranged a short truce with the Kurds, and they gave us back our dead, whom we buried with the full military honors due to brave men. We released our guide.

The next day the Kurds defended one road-block after another, and one after another we outflanked them. If Cheirisophus was held up, I took to the hills, got above the enemy and dislodged them. When the rear guard was attacked, he did the same. It was a model of coöperation. In spite of the weight of our shields and arms, we could climb as well as the Kurds, who carried nothing but their bows and slings—though we could never catch them when they ran away. Our Cretan archers, commanded by Stratocles, were invaluable.

On the evening of November 17th we saw below us at last the plain of the river Centrites. This was an enormous relief, and, as we had plenty of food, we passed a happy night swapping tales about the Kurds and sleeping well. The last seven days had been one long, continuous battle which had cost us more men and suffering than the whole of the fighting with Tissaphernes and the King.

It was just as well that we had time to rest, for the river Centrites did not look so inviting in the morning. On the far bank were cavalry,

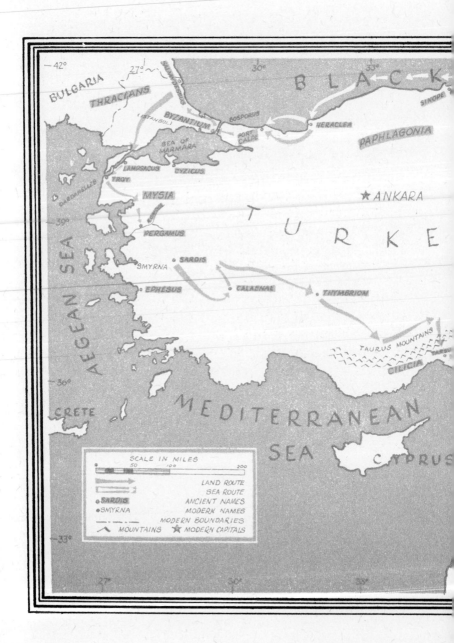

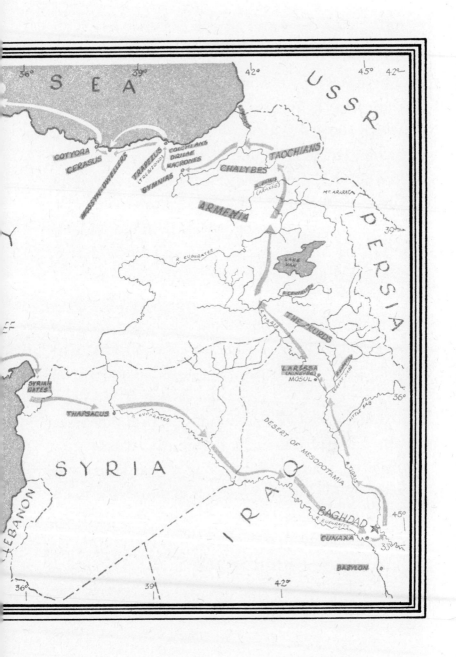

armored from top to toe, to defend the crossing. There was only one way up from the water, and that was a real road, properly engineered, which showed that we were back in civilization again. Drawn up across this road, a hundred yards back from the river, was a powerful force of infantry. These were mostly Chaldean troops who were in the pay of the Imperial Governor of Armenia and were said to be a free, brave people.

We tried the ford, but it was out of the question for heavily armed men. The water was over our chests, and the river bed was of great slippery stones. We hadn't a hope of crossing under fire.

On the edge of the mountains, near our pleasant camp of the night before, the Kurds were massing, ready to fall on our rear as soon as we were in difficulties. We did not know what to do, so we camped where we were for thirty-six hours, feeling that our luck had run out.

That night I had another dream, which was undoubtedly sent from the gods. I dreamed that my legs were chained, that the chains fell off and that I could then stride across anything I wished. As soon as it was dawn, I told this to Cheirisophus, who at once saw the point of it and was delighted. All the generals offered sacrifices, and the appearance of the victims' bodies promised us good fortune.

The troops then had breakfast. While I was eating mine, two young men came running up to me. Everyone knew that I never minded being waked up or having my meals interrupted if the business was military.

The two reported that they had been up the river to collect firewood. On the opposite bank they had seen an old man and some women and little girls storing away bundles of clothing in a hollow rock by the water's edge. The river seemed to be shallow, so the two young fellows undressed and tried the crossing, carrying nothing but their axes. They expected to have to swim at some point; but, to their surprise, the water never quite covered their legs.

Opposite the crossing which they had found,

the foothills of the Armenian mountains fell sharply into the river. On that sort of ground the enemy could not use their cavalry.

I poured out cups of wine for the young men and myself, and we drank to the gods who had saved us and gave them thanks. As soon as Cheirisophus heard the story, he ordered the army to strike camp and fall in for the march. While they were packing up, we generals discussed the coming operation. We decided that Cheirisophus should fight his way over the river with half the army, and that the transport should follow when he had established a bridgehead. Meanwhile, I was to hold our side of the river and watch the Kurds.

We had half a mile to go, and as we marched along the bank the enemy cavalry kept pace with us on the other side. When we arrived at the ford which the young men had discovered, the army halted and piled arms. Then the chaplains held a service and offered sacrifice to the spirit of the river Centrites. Cheirisophus put a ceremonial wreath on his head and threw off his red cloak. The soldiers sang the battle hymn, and the vanguard took to the water in column of companies with Cheirisophus in the center.

As soon as they were on the way over, I called up the fastest troops in the rear guard and raced with them back along the river toward the deep ford with the good road on the other side of it. That drew off the enemy cavalry, who saw that they would be trapped between the hills and the river if both our parties got across.

The threat was quite enough for the Persians, and they bolted. Cheirisophus, now safely over the river, did not pursue them, but swung left and attacked the Chaldean infantry. These weren't going to face the Greek line without any cavalry, so they abandoned their position.

So far all had gone perfectly, but my rearguard was still on the wrong side of the river. Our problem was how to cross it with our defenseless backs exposed to the arrows of the Kurds. I split my force into two—one half to face the river and get the transport over, the other half to form line against the Kurds and attack. When at last this second half was all alone on the bank, it must have seemed to the Kurds a mere handful. They stormed down on us from the hills, chanting their barbarous songs.

Cheirisophus at once sent his archers and slingers to cover the crossing of the last of the rear guard. I ordered them to wait at the ford and hold their fire until we were actually in the water. Then we charged the Kurds and drove them back. At the call of the trumpets we broke off the attack and ran for the river. The Kurds didn't turn and follow us in time; they had had enough of our trumpets and what they meant. When at last they spotted the trick, we were in the middle of the river and under cover of our own archers. And there we were, safely in Armenia, at the expense of only a few men wounded.

CHAPTER 5

Winter

It was now late in November, and the army was up on the highlands of Armenia, somewhere to the west of Lake Van. The physical fitness of the troops must have been far superior to that of modern men. The Greek soldier wore only two garments—a woolen shirt and over it a woolen cloak, rather like a poncho, which left the right arm bare. A few of them, perhaps, had managed to make or loot sheepskin coats, and the leather jackets which they wore in action must have been some protection against the wind. But on the whole they were facing the blizzards which roared down from Russia and the Caucasus in the same clothes that they had worn on the burning plains of Mesopotamia.

The country before us was an open, rolling plain, uninhabited near the Centrites River because of the continual raids of the Kurds. We covered ninety miles in six days and crossed two of the head streams of the Tigris. It was rich country, clustered with large farmhouses walled for defense, and we managed to feed ourselves pretty well.

The governor was a Persian grandee named Tiribazus. When he was in the King's presence, he had the exclusive privilege of helping His Imperial Majesty onto his horse. This personage rode up to our column with an escort of cavalry and told us through an interpreter that he wanted to speak with the commanders. We kept him at a safe distance and accepted the agreement which he offered. He undertook to let us pass through his province in peace and take any supplies we needed; and we on our part promised not to burn down the villages. Then we resumed our march, with Tiribazus' whole army following about a mile behind.

On the third night there was a heavy fall of snow. That was no weather for bivouacking in the open; so at dawn, when we found that Tiribazus and his army had disappeared, we decided to disperse the troops into billets. There were a lot of villages, grouped around a castle, where they could find shelter.

With all that snow outside, it was a great comfort to be under a roof—especially since the houses were full of meat, corn, raisins and vegetables, and old wine of exquisite fragrance. But of course some of our fellows had to come in and say they had seen the blaze of watch fires in the night. So, knowing what we did of Persian treachery, it seemed wiser to give up the billets and concentrate the whole army in the open.

The evening sky was clear and we had no reason to expect more snow. But down it came in the night and covered the piled arms and the sleepers and the transport animals. At reveille nobody wanted to get up, for the snow was like a warm, comfortable blanket except where it slipped off one's shoulders.

Someone had to make a start; so I left my cloak on the ground, jumped up in my shirt and began to split logs for the breakfast fires. Others followed my example, and soon the fires were going and the men were around them, rubbing their bodies with oil. It was local stuff and good, made of pig's lard, oil of sesame and almonds, and turpentine. It had a pleasant smell, and the natives used it for massaging themselves.

We had had enough of the open, and the soldiers yelled with joy when we ordered them back into their billets again. Some of them got poor quarters this time and thoroughly deserved them. They had behaved like savages and set fire to the houses when they were ordered out of them the night before.

It was obvious that we at headquarters could not take any useful action until we knew exactly where Tiribazus was. There was a first-class fellow from Temenon in the army, called Democrates, who had never let us down when we sent him out on reconnaissance. If he reported that something was nonsense, it always was; and if he said we had better look out, he was right. So we sent Democrates off to scout around the hills where the watch fires had been reported.

He came back with the news that there hadn't

been any enemy fires at all and brought with him a prisoner to be questioned. This man was armed with a Persian bow and a battle-ax such as the Amazons are supposed to carry. He said that he was a Persian and had been out on a ration party detailed by Tiribazus. Asked about Tiribazus' army and intentions, he said that the Governor had with him the regular provincial troops and some tribal levies, and that he meant to surprise us in the high pass over the watershed between the Tigris and Euphrates.

That was all the news we needed, and it called for a demonstration in force. We left a strong garrison at headquarters and marched, guided by the prisoner. Tiribazus' camp came in sight as soon as we had crossed the hills, and the light infantry immediately charged down on it without stopping for orders. The enemy didn't wait for the rest of us. We captured twenty horses and Tiribazus' tent with his silver chairs and silver mess equipment and all his butlers and bakers.

The next day we crossed the pass where Tiribazus was to have attacked us, and three days

They pushed through the deep snow for forty-five miles.

On the last march the men were numb and exhausted.

later we came to the river Euphrates—not far, so it was said, from its source—which we forded in water up to the waist.

Now a blizzard began to howl down from the north, and there was no possible shelter from it, as the country was flat. For forty-five miles we plowed through deep snow into the teeth of the wind, and on the last march the men were numbed and exhausted. One of the chaplains then sacrificed to the spirit of the gale, and it was generally agreed that this made a considerable difference.

The snow, however, remained—six feet of it, in which we had to camp. Fortunately there was plenty of wood about, and our great fires ate down to the bare earth. So each party was sitting in a deep hole surrounded by walls of snow.

During the next day's march my rear guard was continually coming up with men who had fallen out of the column and collapsed in the snow. I thought at first that they had been knocked out by disease. But someone who had had experience of extreme cold explained that it was exhaustion, and that if the men got some-

thing to eat they would recover. At once I un-
packed whatever rations there were on the backs
of the transport animals and distributed them.
That put the men on their legs again.

It was dangerous to sit down for any length
of time. I realized how dangerous on one occasion when I was sitting down and waiting for
some men to pack their equipment. I stiffened
all over so quickly that I could not stand. After
that I used to force the men to keep moving
by curses and even blows. We suffered from
snow blindness and frostbite. I found that the
blindness was helped by holding something
black in front of the eyes during the march.
Nothing could be done for frostbite, however,
and many of the men lost their toes. Their feet,
of course, were in shocking condition, for their
sandals had worn out and they were wearing
rough shoes made of untanned ox-hide. If they
slept without taking them off, the shoes froze to
their feet and the strap cut into the flesh.

That night was terrible. We made little progress through the deep snow, and the column
could never get up into whatever camp there

was. Many of our men were dead in the morning. All the time a pack of the enemy were on
our heels, fighting one another for the carcassses
of the transport animals which had dropped
dead, and slaughtering any of our soldiers who
were staggering along behind, numbed or
blinded by cold.

I remember coming upon one party of our
men who had fallen out on a patch of bare
ground where a hot spring had melted the snow.
They could not and would not move, whatever
I did, and begged me to cut their throats and let
them die. We could hear the enemy yapping in
the darkness behind us, arguing and quarreling
over the loot they had picked up.

It was too much. The rear guard turned as if
we were still full of our old spirit, and the men
whose strength was finished shouted as loud
as their poor throats could, and clashed their
shields and spears together. The enemy pan-
icked, and those of them who escaped into the
snow-covered undergrowth were as silent there-
after as those we killed.

The rear guard marched on, assuring the sick

men that a detachment would come out later to bring them in. Then we began to come upon more and more parties lying down in the snow with their cloaks wrapped round them. I sent forward the fittest of my light infantry to find out what was holding up the march. On their return they reported that the whole column was lying down in the snow. We did so, too, without fires and without rations.

At daybreak I ordered back the youngest of the rear guard to bring in the sick and the stragglers. Meanwhile, Cheirisphous was doing the same. He and the vanguard had managed to reach a village where they passed the night, so he had plenty of men fit to march back and carry the helpless into camp. At last we got in all who were alive and billeted them in the nearby villages.

We commanders tossed up for the villages that each contingent should take over. As soon as mine was decided, one of my company commanders, an Athenian named Polycrates, got together a detachment of men who were still active, and surprised the village before the headman and the inhabitants could escape with their property.

That place was just what we needed after such a night. The houses were underground and entered by ladders which led down holes no bigger than the mouth of a well. But inside the dwellings were broad and roomy. Goats, sheep, cattle and poultry all lived underground, too— going in and out by a ramp—and were fed from stacks of green fodder. For us there were wheat, barley, vegetables and barley wine. The natives had an odd way of drinking the wine. It was in big vats filled up to the brim, with the malted grains floating on top. Hollow reeds of all sizes lay on the edge of the vat, and anyone who wanted a drink put in his reed and sucked. It was uncommonly strong, but we found it delicious once we had got used to the taste.

Thanks to Polycrates, who had kept the villagers from running away, we took over the place intact. In it we found, besides all the inhabitants, seventeen colts which were being reared as the tribe's tribute to the Great King. The headman was also there with his daughter, who had been married just eight days before. Her husband was away hunting hare.

I didn't want them to be frightened of us, so I asked the headman to supper, assuring him that his children would be perfectly safe with us, and that when we went away we would fill his house with presents. He was most coöperative and showed us the village cellar where the barley wine was.

The next day he and I made a round of the villages. It was one long party. None of them would let us go until they had served us breakfast—and a breakfast of half a dozen dishes: lamb, kid, pork, veal, fowls and several kinds of bread made of wheat and barley. Their custom of drinking to someone's health was to drag him to the vat and make him lean over it and suck up the barley wine as though he were an ox.

At last we came to Cheirisophus' village. His men were certainly doing well for themselves. They had crowned their heads with garlands of hay and collected a lot of boys in fancy costume. These they were teaching in pantomime how to do the job of civilized waiters. Cheirisophus and

The villagers and their farm animals lived underground.

I greeted each other with somewhat exaggerated affection and then sat down with my tame headman and an interpreter to get a bit of information about the country. We were still in Armenia, he said, and the next tribe we should come to would be the Chalybes.

When I got back to my own village, I took my pick of the colts—since they were the King's property—and gave one each to my fellow-generals and to the officers of my contingent. They were smaller than the Persian horses but much more lively. The headman told me how to get them—and all the transport animals—through the snow. We ought, he said, to wrap sacks around their hoofs and then they would not sink.

We took a week to recover and then resumed our march. I gave the headman whatever useful gifts we could get together and also a horse of mine which could stand no more campaigning. The animal would do, however, for fattening up underground, and the headman, who was a priest of the Sun, could make a sacrifice with it which would honor both him and my horse.

Cheirisophus took my headman with him to guide the army through the snow; and to insure that he didn't play any tricks, we also took his son. On the third day the headman still had not brought us to any villages—there weren't any to bring us to. But Cheirisophus flew into one of his Spartan tempers and beat him up; and my kindly headman ran away in the night, leaving his son with us. That was the only time in the whole march that I ever quarreled with Cheirisophus. We couldn't turn the poor boy loose in the snow, but I am glad to say that Episthenes of Amphipolis, who was in charge of him, had become absolutely devoted to the young fellow. So he took the boy all the way back to Greece and found in him a most faithful friend.

A week's marching at fifteen miles a day brought us to the river Phasis. Soon afterward we came to another range of mountains, and, as usual, the valley we had to follow was barred by a strong force of tribesmen. When Cheirisophus saw them holding the mouth of the pass, he halted three or four miles away and passed the word down the column to deploy for action.

As soon as the rear guard had come up into line, he held a headquarters conference.

"My opinion," he said, showing us the enemy position, "is that we should not tackle that in a hurry. Suppose we let the troops have a meal, and meanwhile discuss whether we ought to attack now or tomorrow?"

Cleanor, the oldest of the commanders, was for immediate action, pointing out that if we waited a day the enemy would grow bolder and probably increase their numbers.

I myself did not like either proposal. Expensive frontal attacks might be all right in their proper place, but our job was to get the army over the range with as few casualties as possible.

"The whole enemy force seems to be concentrated in the pass," I said, "leaving us seven miles of the range to play with. Why not try to find our own way over at night when we won't be seen? Even the stiffest climb is easier than marching on the level and fighting at the same time, and I'm all for a rough road in peace rather than an easy slope with stones and arrows whistling past my ears. What we ought to do is to steal our own bit of mountain and use it.

"That's just the job for you, Cheirisophus," I added. "You're an authority on stealing. I've often heard that you Spartans who belong to the upper class are taught to steal in the military school and whipped if you get caught. Well, there's the mountain! Show us what you can do!"

"Me?" Cheirisophus retorted. "Doesn't everyone know that your politicians in Athens are the biggest thieves in all Greece in spite of what you do to them when you catch them? And as you're always talking about electing the best men to govern you, I suppose you were brought up to imitate them. So let's see if you can steal as well as your politicians, Athenian!"

"All right," I answered, "I'll try. We have some prisoners from the scum that has been raiding the rear guard, and according to them there are cattle grazing on the mountain tops in spite of the steepness and the snow. So if we can take and hold a route, there should be no difficulty in getting the transport animals over."

"No, but seriously, Xenophon," Cheiri-

A Spartan warrior

sophus said, "we can't spare you from the rear guard. Let's call for volunteers to carry out your plan."

We took it easy during the day and at night-fall sent out two detachments of light infantry, with some infantry of the line in support. They occupied a ridge without any trouble and lit fires as a signal to us. We could see that the enemy were alarmed, for they, too, lit a whole lot of fires which they kept blazing all night.

In the morning it was all over very quickly. Our mountain party came down on the flank of the enemy, and we had only to threaten a frontal attack. The tribesmen fled, leaving the pass wide open and throwing away their wicker shields. We picked up a large number of the shields and hacked them to bits with our swords so that they could not be used again. Then we set up a memorial at the top of the pass and marched down the other side into a plain where the army could feed well and rest.

CHAPTER 6

The Sea

It was now about January 1, 400 B.C., and the Greeks were in the foothills of the Caucasus, not far from the present frontier between Turkey and Russia. They had passed right out of the provinces effectively governed by the Persian Empire, and were near the end of the known world.

Still, they were close now to the Black Sea; and where there was sea, there were little, isolated Greek cities. These colonies were independent, but each was bound by close ties of affection to the mother state which had first sent out her adventurers to found it. They were tiny trading towns, with a few square miles of farm

*land outside the walls, set down in the midst of
savages. Generally they were welcome because
of the unheard-of, civilized luxuries which the
tribes and their chieftains could buy in the
Greek markets.*

The next tribe were the Taochians, and in
their country we ran out of food. We never could
get any on the march, for the Taochians took refuge, with all their stores and livestock, in mountain fortresses. These were primitive places
without any houses in them, but they were very
strong.

Cheirisophus tried to storm one of the forts
which was protected on all sides by a ravine. He
could not bring his superior numbers to bear,
so he attacked in three waves on a narrow front,
and all three were beaten back. He was very
glad to see the rear guard when I came up with
it.

"We have to take this infernal place or
starve," he said.

At first sight I couldn't spot the difficulty,
for there seemed to be only a handful of men

against us, and poorly armed at that. I asked him what stopped us from just marching in.

"That crag up there!" he replied. "Every time we go under it, they roll down a load of rocks, and that's what happens." He pointed to some poor fellows with their ribs or legs crushed to bits.

I have always got on very well with Spartans and I admire their discipline enormously, but I must say they do have slow minds.

"Then wait till they have used up all their stones," I said. "Look here! We only have to charge about a hundred and fifty feet, and for the first hundred there is cover behind the trunks of those big pines, at any rate for a few of us. If we can dodge in and out of the trees and draw their fire, they'll soon run out of ammunition."

Cheirisophus and I, with Callimachus, who was officer of the day for the rear guard, went up to the front to control the operation. We managed to get about seventy men, making a dash for it one by one, into the cover of the trees.

Callimachus then hit on a fine trick. He ran forward a few yards from his tree, and when the stones came whizzing down he popped back again. Each of his dashes must have used up ten cartloads of stones. Callimachus' jack-in-the-box act was amusing the whole army, and Agasias, another of my officers, didn't see why he shouldn't have some of the fun. So Agasias made a wild rush for the open, and Callimachus—who wanted to be first into the fort himself—caught him by the shield as he passed. While they were tangled up, two officers who were friends of theirs passed them both. All four got into the fort and captured it.

But there was a horrible end to the comedy. The Taochian women threw their children over the cliff and then themselves. The men followed, and were so anxious to commit suicide that one of them dragged with him an officer who had tried to stop him, and both crashed onto the rocks far below. We took scarcely any prisoners but plenty of cattle, donkeys and sheep.

After the Taochians came the Chalybes. We managed to march 150 miles through their country in a week, but they were the bravest of all the enemies we had met, never hesitating to come to close quarters with our infantry. Their warriors wore helmets, leg armor, and padded tunics to protect the body, and carried spears twenty feet long. They also had short swords, about as long as the Spartan dagger, with which they cut the throat of an opponent when they had him down. Then they would chop off his head and dance with it and sing whenever they knew we were watching.

This tribe, too, had the custom of taking refuge in hill forts. Fortunately we did not have to tackle one. We had enough to eat from the flocks and herds we had captured from the Taochians.

We crossed the river Harpasus and after another 120 miles came to Gymnias—a real city such as we had not seen since we left Babylonia. The ruler of this place gave us a guide—not that he cared what happened to us, but he wanted to let us loose among his enemies. He certainly did; and we had to fight our way, with the guide all the time encouraging us to more fire and slaughter. However, the guide swore on his life

From the mountain they got their first glimpse of the sea.

Wild with joy, the men shrieked and danced like madmen.

that in five days he would take us to a mountain called Thekes, from which we could catch a glimpse of the sea.

On the fifth day we began to march up this mountain. While the rear guard were on the slopes, we heard wild shouting ahead of us, and I thought that the head of the column had walked into trouble. It was likely enough, for the whole country was aflame behind us, and several times the rear guard had had to turn and punish the tribesmen who hung on our tail.

The shouting grew louder and nearer, and detachments began to run up to the front. And the more men who went up, the more noise there was. I still did not guess what had happened and mounted my horse and galloped up to the rescue with the cavalry. Soon I could hear what the soldiers were shouting:

"The sea! The sea!"

Then the rear guard began to run and so did the horses and even the transport animals. When we had all reached the top and set eyes on the distant sea, we embraced one another, generals, officers and men, and the tears ran down our cheeks for joy. Someone or other had the idea of building a monument to mark the spot. So the soldiers brought stones and made a huge mound of them, with skins and posts and captured shields on the top.

After this we sent our guide back to Gymnias with gifts from the common property of the army—a horse, a silver bowl, a Persian dress and ten gold coins. And, since he particularly admired the rings on our fingers, he got a lot of those, too. In the last light of the evening he pointed out to us a village where we could camp and the road on into the territory of the Macrones. Then he turned his back on us and vanished into the night.

We had seen the sea but still had many a hard march before we could reach it. On the third day we found ourselves in a really nasty position and got out of it by a stroke of luck. We were marching down a valley with impossible country to our right and a river on our left. Ahead of us was a tributary river which had to be crossed in spite of a fierce reception committee of Macrones waiting for us on the other side.

While we were cutting down trees to make a causeway, one of my light infantrymen came up to me. He said it was odd, but he seemed to know the language in which the Macrones were chattering.

"I was long a slave in Athens," he explained, "and I think this must be my native country. If you don't mind, sir, I'll try and talk to them."

I was all for it, and told him to go ahead and ask them who they were.

"Macrones," they replied to his question.

"And now ask them why they want to fight us."

"Because you are invading our country," they answered.

"Tell them we don't want their country," I said. "We have been at war with the Great King. We are returning to Greece. And all we want is to reach the sea."

"Will you swear that is the truth, and exchange gifts in the sight of the gods?"

We replied that we certainly would. So the Macrones explained that their solemn custom was to exchange spears. We gave them a Greek spear and received a native lance, and both sides swore to preserve the peace.

After that the Macrones helped us to cut down trees for the crossing and fraternized with us and let us buy whatever they had in their markets. They accompanied us on the march for three days, leaving us when we passed out of their territory into the land of the Colchians.

Here we were faced with a new problem. Our way to the sea led straight up the side of a long range of hills, and on the top were the Colchians drawn up in line of battle. There was no pass and no alternative route.

Headquarters wanted a good old-fashioned battle of line against line, but I wouldn't have it. I said that it was impossible, even for us, to keep formation while climbing, and that we should arrive at the top in any old order. Our line, if we used it, had to be long and thin so that it could not be outflanked, and that meant that the Colchians could charge downhill and break it where they liked. I suggested that we should attack in deep columns, each one to act independently of the rest.

This proposal was carried by a majority of votes, and while the troops were forming up I had a word with them. I told them that the enemies in front of us were the last between us and the sea, and that we were going to eat them raw.

The infantry of the line were in eighty deep columns, with orders to pick their own way up the hill and not to bother about the gaps between them; if the enemy dared to get into these gaps, they would be caught and crushed. On the wings were the light infantry under the command of Cheirisophus and myself. We threatened to outflank the Colchians, who thereupon extended their line to meet us and left a hole in the center of it. Into the hole charged the Arcadians, under the command of our old Cleanor, and that was the end of the battle.

The top of the range was now ours, and we found it thickly inhabited. The people were great beekeepers, and in the villages, among all the usual stores, were astonishing quantities of honeycomb. Its effect was astonishing, too. The soldiers who ate it suffered from violent stomach disorders and loss of balance. Those who had only a little appeared to be incapably drunk, and those who had a lot went mad. There were so many hundreds of them lying on the ground that it looked as if we had just lost a great battle, and we were correspondingly depressed. However, none of them died, and twenty-four hours after eating the honeycomb, almost at the exact moment, they recovered their senses. Three or four days later they could get up, and said they felt as if they had been purged by the most drastic medicine.

When we could move, a march of twenty-one miles in two days brought us to Trapezus. This was one of several little ports pushed out along the coast by the Greek city of Sinope, which itself was a colony of Miletus. We did not want to put too great a strain on the resources of Trapezus, so we billeted ourselves in the native village and raided the surrounding tribes for food.

We stayed here a month, receiving much

kindness from our fellow-Greeks. They opened a market for us, gave us cattle and wheat and wine, and finally made peace between us and the Colchians.

It was now time to fulfill the oath we had taken on that desperate morning after Tissaphernes had assassinated our leaders. We had sworn to offer sacrifice as soon as we reached friendly soil. And there we were at last, with enough cattle—the Colchians, too, had given us some—to make a worthy offering to the gods. So we sacrificed to Zeus the Savior and to Heracles, who guides the lost, and to all the other immortals to whom thanks were due.

When the service and sacrifice were over, we held a sports festival and made Dracontius president. He was a Spartan who had been banished from home ever since he was a boy for having accidentally killed one of his schoolmates with a dagger.

Dracontius was supposed to have chosen a ground for the sports, but when we asked him where it was, he merely waved his hand at the mountain ridge where we were standing. That was a perfectly good place, he said. We could run here, there and everywhere.

"But what about wrestling on this hard ground?" we asked.

"Oh, it will teach the loser not to be thrown," replied our Spartan president.

There was a mile race for boys, most of whom

No holds were barred in the wrestling matches.

were captives we had taken on the march, and a long-distance race, which sixty of our Cretan archers went in for, and wrestling, boxing, and fighting with no holds barred. It was a wonderful show because there were lots of entries for every event and the enthusiasm of the spectators, men and women, was immense.

There was a horse race, too—or what Dracontius thought was one. We had to gallop down the steep hill to the sea, turn around in the water and come up again to the finishing post, which was the altar where we had held our sacrifice. Going down the hill, half of us went over our horses' heads, and on the way back the horses toiled up the slope in a walking race. It made a grand finale. You should have heard the shouting, the laughter and the cheers!

At the end of the day we held a meeting of the whole army to decide what we were to do next. The first speaker was Antileon of Thurii.

"Gentlemen," he said, "I'm tired of packing my stuff. I'm tired of parades. I'm tired of quick marching and double marching and carrying this heavy shield and spear. I'm tired of forming line and guard duties and battles. And now that I have the sea in front of me, what I'm going to do is to lie on my back on a deck and wake up to find myself in Greece."

The men naturally cheered this, and several others got up and spoke to the same effect. In fact there wasn't a soul who disagreed with Antileon. Even Cheirisophus was a bit of an optimist on this occasion.

"Gentlemen," he said, "by a stroke of luck there's a friend of mine commanding the Spartan fleet at the naval base of Byzantium. His name is Anaxibius, and if you would like to send me to him, I think I can promise to return with enough ships to carry us. Meanwhile, all you have to do is to wait here."

Of course it was voted that Cheirisophus should set off at once, and everyone assumed that our troubles were over. It was left to me to put a bit of common sense into the meeting.

"Splendid!" I told them. "We have all agreed to await Cheirisophus' return. But what are we going to eat meanwhile? You'll have to fight for your food, whether you like it or not, so we had better preserve some discipline. Now, this is what I propose:

"First, you are not to go wandering off to forage on your own. The organization of ration parties must be left to headquarters.

"Second, you will be raiding enemy country, and must expect reprisals. Therefore, guard duties will go on as at present.

"Third, it is not at all certain that Cheirisophus can persuade Anaxibius to give us enough ships, so we ought to borrow a warship from Trapezus and capture some of our own.

"Fourth, in case we don't get any ships at all, we must persuade the colonies to make us roads for a march along the coast. They'll be only too glad to do it to get rid of us."

The army accepted all my proposals except the last, which they howled down. They had had enough of marching. But as a matter of fact I put this point quietly to Trapezus and to the other colonies when we came to them, and they set the roads in order at once, just as I had said they would.

A few days later Cheirisophus set off. After he had gone, we borrowed a fifty-oar galley from Trapezus, giving the command of it to Dexippus, a Laconian. This scoundrel made off with the ship. I'm glad to say that in the end he was executed for engaging in some sort of underhand business with the native princes of Thrace—but not before he had caused us more trouble.

Then we borrowed a thirty-oar galley and this time made the Athenian Polycrates captain. He laid his hands on a number of the vessels which used to sail past Trapezus, and we commandeered them. We didn't want to get the reputation of pirates, so we stacked the cargoes on the beach under guard, and we paid the crews out of the common army funds.

Meanwhile, we were eating up all the food in the country and had to go far afield to get more. The people of Trapezus naturally did not want us to set the coastal natives against them. So they showed us the way into the mountains and told us to go and raid the Drilae—one of the most warlike tribes on the Black Sea coast, with inaccessible fortresses. We had heavy fighting, heavy losses and mighty little food.

At the end of March, when Cheirisophus had still not returned, there was only one thing to do. We had to march again. We had enough ships to carry the surplus baggage and the boys, women, invalids, and veterans over forty. The rest of us tramped eastward along the coast. On the third day we all met at Cerasus, another port belonging to Sinope, and held a review of the army. There were 8,600 of us left out of the 13,000 who had fought at Cunaxa.

We also settled up the accounts for the Persian and tribal prisoners whom we had sold as slaves. Before distributing the prize money, we set aside one-tenth for a thank-offering to Apollo and Artemis. The generals were entrusted with this money and were to spend it as they wished in the service of the gods.

Out of my portion I gave a piece of plate to the temple of Apollo at Delphi, inscribed with my name and that of Proxenus. The money which was dedicated to Artemis I spent long afterward in the place where I am writing—Scillus, close to Olympia.

CHAPTER 7

Discipline Breaks Down

The army's problem was how to get along the coast of what is now Turkey all the way from Cerasus to the Bosporus. It could be done only by sea. But the Greek colonies were terrified by this force of hungry, powerful, hard-bitten adventurers. The generals' only chance of getting ships was by clever diplomacy and good behavior.

At Cerasus the army began to get out of hand. There were quarrels in the market and a bad case of a private raid on a town which ended in defeat. Worse still, when three old men were sent by the town to try to clear the matter up in a friendly spirit, the army stoned them to death. When we left Cerasus, we had the reputation of a bunch of hoodlums.

Our few ships coasted along as before, while we of the land party had to cross the territory of the Mossyn-dwellers, whose chieftains live in high wooden towers called Mossyns. They had fair hair and white skins, but they were the most primitive, barbarous people we had met in the whole of our march.

The Mossyn-dwellers had a sort of consul at Trapezus, a Greek called Timesitheus who looked after their trade with the colony. He very kindly came with us and tried to persuade the Mossyn-dwellers to allow us to march through their country.

When they flatly refused, Timesitheus, who of course was well informed on the local politics, told us that the country was in a state of civil war. He said that the tribesmen farther to the west would probably help us against the eastern part of their nation, which was holding us up.

He sent for the western chiefs, and we had a conference with them. I explained that we were on our way home to Greece, and that we had no intention of staying. If the chiefs wanted to wipe out their enemies, I said, this was their chance, for they would never see such a powerful force again.

The chiefs eagerly agreed and promised to send us ships, men and guides. The ships turned up the next day. They were dugout canoes—300 of them—each holding three men. Of these, one paddled the canoe away, while the other two landed. Then the men on shore staged a war dance.

They stood opposite one another in two lines, just like the chorus in our Greek theater. All of them had shields of cowhide on a wicker frame, shaped like an ivy leaf. They carried spears nine feet long with a point at one end and a knob, carved from the wood, at the other. They also had battle-axes. They wore linen shirts down to their knees and leather helmets with tufts of hair like the points of a crown.

After their dance one of them sang out a key-note and the rest started chanting. Then they pranced right through our infantry without pay-

Standing opposite one another, the

ing any attention to them and marched straight on a fortress which defended the approach to their capital.

The capital contained the highest of the wooden towers, built on the top of the citadel. In the tower their king lived as a sort of sacred prisoner, whose court was kept going by all the tribe in common. That was the cause of the civil war. The eastern Mossyn-dwellers had claimed that they alone had the right to the tower and the king.

men on shore staged a war dance.

Our army had no orders to join in this attack; but some of the soldiers, hoping for loot, broke away and followed the savages. The defenders of the fortress easily repulsed the assault, and those Greeks who had acted without orders ran for their lives—the first time that such a thing had happened in the whole history of the expedition.

I had to say something about this disgrace, which shocked us all very much. I pointed out that it had only happened through lack of dis-

cipline and said we must at once show the
friendly Mossyn-dwellers that running away was
not a habit of ours. We must prove to the
enemy, I insisted, that we were very different
soldiers from any they had ever known.

The next day we sacrificed and found that our
luck was good. Then we staged the operation as a
model job: infantry of the line in columns;
archers and light infantry in the gaps and well
forward; savages on the left flank. The enemy
met us at the same fortress and managed to hold
the light infantry, but the line simply marched
right over them and on to the capital.

The Mossyn-dwellers defended the houses
very obstinately, hurling their nine-foot spears
and using long ones, almost too heavy for a man
to lift, to hold us off at close quarters. When
they found that this time the weight of our attack continually increased instead of weakening,
they abandoned the capital. The king refused to
come out of his wooden Mossyn and so did those
who were left in the first fortress after it had
been overrun. They all perished in the flames.

We raided the town supplies for our food and

found bread, stacks of wheat in the stalk and jars of pickled dolphin in slices. There were also jars of dolphin fat, which the Mossyn-dwellers use just as we do oil, and quantities of sweet chestnuts which they eat boiled and whole, and grind into flour for loaves. Their wine was rough but tasted all right when mixed with water.

After handing over the town to our strange allies, we marched on westward and met no more resistance. The country was all peaks and deep valleys, and, though the hilltop settlements averaged ten miles from one to another, the inhabitants could shout and be heard across the intervening space. The friendly part of the tribe entertained us in some of these settlements. They liked to show us the children of their wealthy families, who were deliberately fattened on a diet of boiled chestnuts so that they were nearly as broad as they were tall. Their skin was very white and delicate and tattooed all over with patterns of flowers.

Their customs astonished us. Anything that a Greek would prefer to do in privacy, they loved to do in a crowd. And, when alone, a Mossyndweller would carry on as if he were in company, talking to himself and laughing and capering just as if he were showing off to an audience.

We were eight days in this country. Then, passing through two smaller tribes in peace, we arrived at Cotyora, another of Sinope's colonies. We were badly received there, for the town would not accept our sick and wounded or give us any opportunity to buy food. Consequently, we were forced to take what we wanted.

This alarmed the city of Sinope, which at once sent a delegation to us headed by a very eloquent politician called Hecatonymus. He said all the right things, expressing the pride of Sinope in our victories and their thankfulness that we had arrived safely on the coast. Then he protested, still very politely, against our treatment of Cotyora and suggested that if we didn't behave ourselves, Sinope would turn the Paphlagonians loose on us. They were the nation whose territory surrounded Sinope.

This sort of diplomacy was just what we were brought up on in Athens, so the army asked me to reply.

Now fortunately the city of Trapezus had been so pleased with our treatment of them—and of their enemies—that they had provided us with some of their own citizens as guides. These were still with us, and I told the delegates from Sinope to ask them what sort of people we were.

"And here are all the crimes we have committed," I said. "When Cotyora would not sell us food, we took it, and we are still willing to pay for it. When they closed their gates and refused to admit our sick, we just walked in where their walls were weak and found hospital accommodation and paid the expenses. I admit that we then posted a guard on the city gates, but only to insure that our invalids were not ill-treated and that we could remove them when we wished.

"The rest of us, as you can see, are camping in the open in regular military lines. Do we look to you an undisciplined mob? No, we look ready for anything—ready, if we must, to take on both you and the Paphlagonians. But it would suit us much better to ally ourselves with the Paphlagonians—and they, I hear, might be quite glad to get rid of Sinope."

This put the delegates in a panic. They insisted that the last thing they wanted was war. No, they had only come to demonstrate their affection for us. They were certain that every word I said was true. As for Hecatonymus (who got a lot of unpleasant looks from his fellow-delegates), what he had meant was that if they had to choose between us and the Paphlagonians, they would choose Greeks every time.

After that there was no more trouble with Cotyora or Sinope. We were treated to gifts and dinner parties and much delightful conversation.

Hecatonymus told us that to march through Paphlagonia was more than difficult—it was absolutely impossible. The mountain passes were mere slits in the rock, and, when we came to the plains, we should be up against a mass of cavalry of far better quality than that of the Persians. He was obviously telling the truth, since it was in Sinope's interest that we should go on by land. If we didn't, they would have to provide the ships.

We talked this over among ourselves, and the

army voted in favor of going by sea, provided we could get enough ships from Sinope and Heraclea to take us all at once. It was no good leaving a fraction of the army behind. They would soon find themselves reduced to starvation and sold into slavery.

We sent delegates to the two cities to ask for ships. Meanwhile, the army waited at Cotyora, bored and inactive. Every day I saw camped around me this magnificent, well-balanced force of hardened veterans, and I could not help thinking what a fine colony we could found on the eastern shore of the Black Sea. I did not dare breathe a word of this to the army, but I sent for Silanus, a most experienced army chaplain whose advice to Cyrus had been remarkably accurate; and asked him to perform a sacrifice and see what the gods wished. I made him do it in my presence, since by this time I was myself quite good at reading the future from the appearance of the carcasses.

Silanus said that the signs were all in favor of my colony, but that it looked as if I would be cheated out of it by some conspiracy. He told the truth, too, for the conspirator was himself. He had no interest in being stuck in a Black Sea colony, so he went off to his friends and gave the whole scheme away.

There was a fearful row. I was really in some danger from the troops. Fortunately our delegates came back with a definite promise of ships. So I was able to say, quite honestly, that if we had them and if we could all move together I saw no more point in founding a colony.

But no sooner had that unpleasantness blown over than I was in trouble again. Some of my fellow-commanders changed their minds and began to think the colony would be a good idea. That, of course, was put down to my bad influence. Then the soldiers got it into their heads that when they were on board the ships, we should give orders for the fleet to sail east instead of west. They got completely out of hand. I had to call a meeting and explain, at the risk of my life, that what they feared was impossible. They had only to look at sunrise and sunset to see which way the fleet was sailing.

When all this was over, we were ashamed of

ourselves. As one man the whole army voted that mutinous behavior would have to stop, and that the ringleaders should be punished. We set up courts-martial to deal with any crimes that had been committed since the death of Cyrus. And on my strong recommendation, backed by the chaplains, we held a service of repentance and absolution.

The generals, too, had to face a court of inquiry. Two were fined because the cargoes we had taken off the captured ships and placed under guard were found to have been pilfered. Another was fined for neglect of duty. I myself was charged with common assault on private soldiers.

I asked my chief accuser to state where and when I had beaten him.

"When we were dying of cold in the deep snow," he said.

"Probably guilty," I admitted. "But I don't recognize you. Are you a soldier of the line?"

"No."

"Light infantryman?"

"No."

"What, then?"

"Mule driver."

"Ah, yes," I said. "Of course you're the fellow I ordered to load a dying man." And I told the court what really happened. "The rear guard found this man digging a hole to bury a fellow-soldier. While I stood by, the soldier kicked, and we all exclaimed that he was alive.

" 'Alive or not,' said this mule driver, 'I won't carry him. He's going to die.'

" 'So are we all,' I answered. 'But that's no reason why we should be buried alive.'

"And then I beat him up."

After that, the jury was all for me, and none of my accusers dared to say a word. However, I wanted this question cleared up for good, so I went on to speak in my own defense.

"In that deadly cold I beat men for their own sake," I said. "And I have beaten men, too, when they left the line in action to go and loot. And I may have used force on stragglers to save them from being overtaken by the enemy and lanced. My defense is simple. I claim that I am no more deserving of punishment than a parent or school-master who smacks a child.

"Or do you think it was sheer brutality? If you do, I ask you to remember that I am a stronger man than I was and a good deal tougher, and I drink a lot more wine. So if brutality were in my character, you would expect it to come out now. But it does not, and why? Because when a ship is in smooth water at last, there is no need for the helmsman to curse and carry on as he did when it was in danger.

"Gentlemen of the jury, when I drove the rear guard through the snow, you did not have voting papers in your hands. You had swords. If you did not approve of my methods, there was the remedy!

"You remember now the times when you hated me. But were there no times when I eased for you the agony of storm and winter or turned on the enemy or helped you in sickness and want? Did I not praise every gallant deed and see that the doer was honored by us all? All this is forgotten. But isn't it more just, more kindly, more in accordance with the divine will and pleasanter, too, to remember good rather than evil?"

This started up many a memory of comradeship in the jury, and the court rose in a far happier mood than any of us had reason to expect.

The ships arrived, and we sailed for a day and a night along the coast of Paphlagonia. On May 20th we reached Sinope, which gave us a magnificent reception with 4,500 bushels of barley and 1,500 jars of wine.

Here Cheirisophus at last rejoined us. To our disappointment he brought nothing but a single warship and the empty congratulations of his friend, the Spartan admiral Anaxibius.

Our next port of call was Heraclea, only 120 miles from the entrance to the Bosporus. We were now nearly in Greek waters, and the army began to think what a pity it was to return home without a penny in our pockets. They held meetings and came to the conclusion that they would like to appoint a commander in chief who would lead them on a last expedition. They were tired of being commanded by a headquarters conference, whose decisions were slow and always leaked out and caused trouble.

They asked me to take the job, and I was very eager to accept it—though it was as likely to lead me to ruin as to fame. Under these difficult circumstances I performed a sacrifice to Zeus the King, to whom I had been told to pray by the priestess at Delphi when I made my pilgrimage before setting out on the expedition.

To my great disappointment the god told me clearly that I should not ask for the supreme command or accept it if it was offered.

So, when I was put up for election at a general meeting of the army, I refused. I told them that they ought to elect a Spartan. The Spartans were the leaders of all the states of Greece, and it would be intolerable for them to find that, after their victory over Athens, so powerful an army was in the hands of an Athenian.

My friend Agasias—he who had taken the Taochian fort—said this was ridiculous. Were the Spartans to take offense because a lot of friends held a dinner party and didn't ask a Spartan to sit at the head of the table?

"If that's how they are going to look at it," he said, "I don't see why we Arcadians are allowed to be officers at all."

This raised a laugh against the Spartans, and I had to confess my real reasons—how I had sacrificed and received a sign so plain that even a man with no religious training could not fail to understand it.

The meeting then elected Cheirisophus. He thanked the army and said that, though he would have backed me most loyally, Anaxibius and the Spartans did distrust me and I was very wise not to have accepted the command. He ordered the army to sail the next day for Heraclea.

CHAPTER 8

Back to Europe

Nobody knew what this international army would or would not do. It was not responsible to any government at all. Worse still, it obeyed men who could make any amount of trouble for the Spartans—this adventurous Athenian Xenophon and despised Arcadians like old Cleanor and the fiery Agasias. The Spartans could hardly leave fellow-Greeks to starve; but at the same time they did not like the thought of a first-class army outside Byzantium.

Byzantium was the first name of the city which was later called Constantinople and is now Istanbul. Then, as now, it commanded the entrance to the Black Sea. It was originally a col-

ony of the Athenians and had been taken from them by the Spartans a few years before Xeno-phon's expedition.

We anchored at Heraclea, off a peninsula where Heracles is said to have descended to the lower world to fetch the dog Cerberus. The cleft he entered, 1,300 feet deep, is still shown to tourists.

Heraclea provided us with only three days' food and offered no reasonable suggestions for getting any more. The army was angry and held a meeting at which it was decided that Cheirisophus and I should go up to the city and demand a lump sum of money. We both flatly refused to blackmail Heraclea, and the army thereupon sent a delegation of its own, consisting of Agasias and two other officers. They were far from tactful, however, and the result was what I expected. The citizens of Heraclea carried into the town all their property and stores from the farms round about, closed the gates and manned the walls with their fighting men.

That was that. And there was such bitter

feeling in the army that the Arcadians and Achaeans, who supplied the majority of our infantry of the line, declared that they were not going to obey a Spartan and an Athenian any longer. They broke away and formed an independent force. So Cheirisophus' supreme command lasted barely a week.

The only way to get food was to raid the Bithynians who lived behind Port Calpe. This was a good harbor midway between Heraclea and Byzantium. The country inland was rich, but it had never been colonized. Ships passed Port Calpe far out, for the Bithynians had a reputation for savage treatment of any Greek crews who fell into their hands.

The Arcadians were the first to move. Heraclea had given them some ships to get rid of them. Four thousand they were, all infantry of the line. Cheirisophus, ill and disappointed that he had lost his command, marched along the coast with 2,000 of the remainder; and I, also with 2,000, made a circuit inland. I had our little force of cavalry—now about forty troopers.

The cavalry soon brought in word that some disaster had happened to a Greek force, and we hurried to the rescue. To make my little army appear much larger than it was, I extended the men over the country as far as was safe and set fire to everything inflammable. At night we lit more watch fires than were needed, so that all the plain and mountains seemed to be blazing.

What had occurred was that the Arcadians had landed and marched into the interior. This was sheer folly, for they hadn't a single archer or light infantryman. When the Bithynians attacked them, they were shot to pieces and could not retaliate. The Arcadians were then driven to take refuge on an isolated hill, where they were surrounded and cut off from water.

Fortunately we were in time. The Bithynians were alarmed by our fires and retreated. In the morning we relieved the Arcadians, and then all of us marched back to Port Calpe together. There we found Cheirisophus' army under the command of Neon. Cheirisophus was dead. He had been marching with a fever, and he died of the too drastic drugs which he took to cure himself.

Agasias and other Arcadian officers, now thoroughly ashamed of themselves and their heavy losses, called a meeting of their troops, which voted that anyone who suggested splitting up the army should be punished with death, and that the former generals should be reinstated.

Back under the old headquarters and with a properly balanced force in hand, we were able to smash the Bithynians. Then we settled down at Port Calpe for the month of July and made a sort of temporary colony of it. The country produced everything we needed except olives, and the army managed to accumulate some surplus funds for buying food. Once the trading captains knew that Port Calpe was in safe hands, all the ships which passed along the coast began to put in and sell to us.

We were getting along very well when Cleander, the Spartan Governor of Byzantium, arrived with a couple of warships. He was accompanied by Dexippus, the man who had

The Spartan Governor arrived with several warships.

stolen the fifty-oar ship which we borrowed from Trapezus.

Unfortunately there was no responsible person in the camp to receive the Governor. The entire army was out on maneuvers except for a small ration party who had just come in with a flock of sheep. This was Dexippus' chance to make trouble and get Cleander on his side. So he accused the ration party of intending to keep the sheep for themselves instead of putting them into the common stock of the army. He arrested one of the soldiers, who belonged to Agasias' company, and tried to take him to Cleander.

When the army turned up, Agasias at once rescued his man, and the troops with him stoned Dexippus amid yells of "Traitor!" Cleander and his crews were scared by the uproar and took refuge on board their ships.

My fellow-generals and I apologized. But Cleander was ashamed of his retreat—all the same, it was no joke to face our army when it was angry—and in a furious temper. He threatened to return to Byzantium and to issue a proclamation declaring us public enemies and forbidding any city to receive us. We implored him not to be so cruel, but he would agree only on condition that Agasias and his man were surrendered to him for execution.

There was nothing to do but to call a meeting of the whole army. Some of the speakers were inclined to take Cleander's threat far too lightly. I had to remind them of the Spartan power. Cleander and Admiral Anaxibius could prevent us ever getting home by blockading us where we stood.

Agasias, who was a particular friend of mine and always a sportsman, solved the problem by getting up and saying that he was going to give himself up to Cleander. He asked only that we send a delegation with him because he was not very good at finding words to defend himself.

But he did not do at all badly. He boldly took full responsibility for the attack on Dexippus and gave Cleander the story of the man's treachery. If it had been Cleander himself who had arrested his soldier, he would never, he said, have resisted. But he wasn't going to allow Dexippus to get away with it.

Cleander was obviously disgusted by Dexippus' conduct, but he refused to yield. He said that however great a scoundrel Dexippus was it was no excuse for violence, and that he proposed to put an end to it once and for all.

When Cleander had eaten his lunch and calmed down, we tried him again. Dracontius, the respectable old Spartan who had run our sports, led the delegation; but I, of course, had to do most of the talking. The essential thing was to persuade Cleander that all the scandal he had heard about us and his unlucky first impression of us were wrong, and that we really were a disciplined force.

I told him that we would accept his judgment, whatever it was, and treat it with the utmost respect. All we asked was that he take into consideration the services which Agasias and his company had rendered to the army and weigh them against the worth of Dexippus.

"And if you want to see what sort of men we are," I said, "take command of us! We promise to serve you loyally and to show you how we can obey and how we fight."

Then Cleander jumped up and swore by the twin gods of Sparta that all he had heard about us was nothing but lies.

"Take Agasias and his man," he cried. "And I myself will accept the command of your army and lead you back to Greece."

From that time on, Cleander and I trusted each other; and much misery and misunderstanding could have been avoided if only he had been our commander in chief. But the gods were against it. It did not matter how many times we sacrificed; no sort of luck was promised to him if he took the command.

"Go forward then," he said at last, "with the generals who have led you so far and who will bring you home. And have no fear when you come to Byzantium! You will be welcome."

Anaxibius provided ships and promised us pay; and we all crossed over the Bosporus to Byzantium. Once there, I felt that my duty was done and proposed to sail home to Athens. When, however, I called at the Governor's residence to say good-bye to Cleander, he advised me not to embark just yet.

"If you do," he said, "you will be blamed because the army is unwilling to leave the city."

"I don't see why I should be," I answered. "The reason why the army does not want to go and camp in the open country is that they haven't any food or money; and Anaxibius has neither paid us nor made a single practical suggestion."

"I know," said Cleander. "But people are going to say that you incited your men to make as much trouble as possible and then cleared out. Take my advice, and help us to get the army outside the walls before you leave."

"All right," I agreed. "Then come with me to Anaxibius' office."

Anaxibius was thoroughly unhelpful. He said that he had issued an order that the army was to leave the city, and that he was going to see it was obeyed. We were to bring our full strength in review, number the men and march out; and any absentees would have to take the consequences.

I didn't argue. We marched out of Byzantium in active service order, with full equipment and transport animals, and the generals at the head of the column.

Then, when we were out and the gates closed, this intolerable Anaxibius summoned us and our officers before him. He told us to supply ourselves as best we could from the villages of Thrace and to get out of Byzantine territory without delay.

So the troops, far from being at the end of

their troubles, were expected to march home around the north of the Aegean, fighting hostile tribes for their food. As soon as the news reached them, they mutinied. Some of them battered on the gates and threatened to split them wide open. Others ran along the breakwater and over the sea walls into the city. Then a bunch who had never come in review and had thus remained within the walls seized the gates and flung them open.

This meant disaster for us all, and I could only hope that the troops would obey me. I plunged into the crowd and was swept through the gates into the city. The Byzantines were in a panic and trying to launch their ships to escape. The garrison had retreated into the citadel. Anaxibius took a fishing boat and joined them and at once ordered up all troops available on the Asiatic shore.

Meanwhile, the troops recognized me and mobbed me.

"Now then, Xenophon," they shouted, "show yourself the sort of man we want! Here's a city

Xenophon was swept through the gates into the city.

and ships and money and your own army! Take over the lot, and we'll make you famous!"

The crowd of mutineers was in the Thracian Square, a fine, level, open space for a drill ground.

"If that's what you want," I answered, "then —Army of Cyrus, fall in! Light infantry, to the flanks! Line, into eights, form column!"

They obeyed automatically. And then I gave them the orders:

"Pile arms! Stand easy!"

That made them an army again, and an army to whom one could talk.

"Soldiers," I said, "I share your anger at the monstrous way we have been swindled. I, too, would like to take vengeance and plunder the city. But have you thought of the consequences? It will mean war with the Spartans and with their allies.

"Remember what happened to Athens— Athens with three hundred ships of war, with treasure such as no other city of Greece ever knew, with the islands and the ports of Asia Minor as allies, and even this city of Byzantium.

You know that in the end we were utterly defeated. What do you think the chance of this army would be?

"And it is not as if you would have to fight only the Spartans. Athens and all the old allies of Athens are now with them. And even if you made a stand in Asia and held them off, what of the Great King and Tissaphernes, who are aching for revenge against us?

"No! We must try to obtain justice in some other way but war. My advice to you is to send a message to Anaxibius that you have no intention of harming the city. Tell him that we have entered it only in despair and that, if he still will not help us, we shall be sure at least that he means his decision and that it is final. We know what discipline means. We will march and go."

They sent the message, and Anaxibius answered like a prig that the army would never regret discipline and that he would give a good report of them at home. Those were all the thanks we got for our good behavior. And as soon as we had left the city, he closed the gates and issued a proclamation that any of our men found inside should be put up for auction and sold as slaves.

When the army had settled into camp and the men were quiet, I asked Cleander if I might have a pass to enter Byzantium, as I wanted to find a ship and sail home. Cleander came out to see me and said he had had a most difficult interview with the Admiral. Anaxibius would allow me into the city only on condition that I left with him in his own ship. That was not what I would have chosen, but I accepted and said my last good-byes to the army.

But, after all, I was not destined to part from them yet. Anaxibius' ship crossed the Sea of Marmara to Cyzicus. There he met the Spartan, Aristarchus, who was on his way to Byzantium to relieve Cleander as governor. Aristarchus also gave us the news that Anaxibius had been ordered home.

Now all along our old enemies, the Persians, had been intriguing with the Spartans, unknown to us. It turned out that Anaxibius had not ferried us over from Asia to Europe from any love of the army. He did so because Pharnabazus, the Great King's governor on the Marmara coast, had offered him a bribe to get us out of his province.

Anaxibius, as soon as he heard that he had lost his command, tried to collect his money from Pharnabazus. But Pharnabazus, who had also heard the news, refused to give him a cent. Thereupon Anaxibius suddenly became patriotic and decided to keep together and even to send back into Asia the army which had so frightened the Persians.

It was certain that the army would be ready enough to fight Persians and collect some really useful loot, but the only person who could control it was myself. So Anaxibius played on my feelings. It was easy. I cared nothing for politics but only for my beloved troops. So I consented to go back at once. Anaxibius laid on a thirty-oar galley to take me across the Sea of Marmara, and had relays of horses and an escort waiting on the other side. I received a wildly enthusiastic welcome from the army, which had been experimenting with all sorts of unlikely commanders, and I began to prepare for the crossing to Asia and the campaign against Pharnabazus.

I found that the army was breaking up. Some of the men had sold their arms and bought themselves passages home to Greece; and some had decided to settle in the colonies around Byzantium. In Byzantium itself there wasn't one of our men left. Cleander had refused to sell any of them into slavery and had even taken a personal interest in the care of our sick and wounded. But as soon as Aristarchus arrived, he brutally put the whole lot up for auction.

He, of course, was now hoping to get the fat bribe which Pharnabazus had promised to Anaxibius. So he refused to allow us to cross over to the Asiatic shore and threatened to sink our transports if we tried it. And then he attempted to decoy me into the city, with the intention of arresting me and handing me over to Pharnabazus. Meanwhile, the army, as usual, was moneyless and very short of food.

CHAPTER 9

The Last Adventure

The Greeks were the only civilized people in eastern Europe, but there were tribes in the Balkans who were allied to them in blood and slowly absorbing their culture. Among these were the Thracians, who lived in what is now Bulgaria. The army found them barbarous, but their customs were fairly familiar. There were many Thracian soldiers in the light infantry.

For some time a Thracian prince named Seuthes had been making offers to the army. They had never seemed to me very attractive, but now, with another winter coming on, we had to consider them.

One night I took with me representatives from all the contingents of the army and rode to Seuthes' camp. The Prince was very nervous. He had taken up his quarters in a tower, surrounded by an alert and powerful force of guards. All his horses were bitted and bridled ready for instant escape.

After we had drunk a bowl of wine together, I asked him what he wanted the army for. He said that he had a right to the overlordship of all the Thracian tribes but that after the king, his father, died, he had been reduced to living as an outlaw and raiding the land that ought to be his. With the help of our army he hoped to recover his inheritance.

He promised one gold piece a month to the men, two to the officers and four to the generals. He also undertook to give us refuge and land if we got into trouble with the Spartans. And then he offered to marry me to his daughter and to take mine, if I had one, for his own wife.

When I returned to the army with Seuthes' terms, they accepted them. We marched to join him at once, and he led us to villages where there was plenty of food.

The very afternoon of our arrival the Prince invited all the officers to dine with him. Before we went in, we were all approached by a certain Heracleides—a Greek adventurer in Seuthes' service—who told us that it was the custom of the country to bring the Prince a present. This was a shock. Personally I had no possessions in the world but one slave boy and enough money to pay my mess bill.

The dinner was good in a primitive way. Three-legged tables were scattered about the hall, and on them were placed piles of meat, with loaves of bread attached to the roasts by great skewers. Seuthes started to carve at the table in front of him and then threw the pieces and the bread to his guests, keeping very little for himself. This seemed to be the polite custom of the country, so each of us who was seated before a table did the same for those who were not.

Among us was an Arcadian officer called

Seuthes started to carve and then threw

Arystas, who had an enormous appetite. He soon got tired of playing catch with little bits of meat, so he grabbed a huge loaf with a roast skewered to it, put it on his knee and settled down. When the wine was served, he waved it away.

"Can't you see I'm busy?" he said to the butler. "Give it to Xenophon, who has nothing better to do."

This amused Seuthes—and it was just as well, for now came the time when he expected his presents.

the pieces and the bread to his guests.

A Thracian strode in leading a white horse and gave it to the Prince with a pretty speech and drank his health. Another gave a slave; another, clothes for the Prince's wife. Timasion, one of our new generals, managed to produce a silver bowl and a Persian carpet. Gnesippus, an Athenian who was as penniless as myself, said boldly that it was a fine custom to present gifts to a king, and so he hoped the King would soon make him rich enough to have something to give.

It was now my turn to drink Seuthes' health

and make my gift, and as I was sitting next to him at the high table, I was very embarrassed. However, I had been dining pretty well and was just in the mood for an after-dinner speech. So I got up and said that I presented the prince with myself and the army and his own lands.

This went over very well. Seuthes made a loving cup of the wine on our table and drained it with me.

Then we had music on trumpets made of cowhide. Seuthes himself performed a war dance, and a party of Thracian clowns came tumbling in to amuse us. When dinner was over, we took the field that very night.

In our first few days of campaigning we captured for Seuthes 12,000 head of livestock and 1,000 slaves. He sent Heracleides down to the coast with all this loot, in order to sell it and get pay for the army.

It was now late in December, and, though we were always camped on low ground, we found the weather bitterly cold. The wine and the drinking water used to freeze, and many of us had noses and ears frostbitten. By watching the

Thracians, we understood at last how we ought to dress for winter. They wore fox-skin caps over head and ears, and shirts that covered their legs. When on horseback they folded around them long cloaks which came down to the feet instead of our short cavalry capes.

Our force was so overwhelming that we had very little fighting. The tribesmen took to the mountains and left to us all the riches of the plain. Seuthes, however, was too confident, and one night he put the Greek headquarters in a big village right under the hills. The Thracians attacked, and were guided by villagers to the houses where we were sleeping. They hurled themselves at the doors and dealt with our spears in a most original way, trying to knock the heads off with clubs.

They knew me by name and concentrated their attack on my billet, shouting:

"Come out, Xenophon, and die fighting, or be roasted alive!"

It looked as if we should be roasted, for they had fired the roof. But our eighteen-year-old trumpeter then blew the rally, and we charged out fully armed and using our short swords. The Thracians ran, slinging their shields behind them to protect their backs. As they climbed over the fence around the village, many of their shields got caught on the stakes So we had our revenge. Not one of our men was killed, but some who could ill afford it had their equipment and clothing burned.

We had now been in Seuthes' service for over a month, but the soldiers got only twenty days' pay. Heracleides said that he had not been able to sell the loot for any more.

I told him frankly that he was not doing his duty to Seuthes and that he ought to have come back with the full pay even if he had to borrow it. After all, Seuthes was in no position to collect taxes, and he would never have any money unless Heracleides used his superior intelligence.

This made him very angry, and from then on I was between two fires. Heracleides told his Prince that I was too fond of the troops to be a good general, and the troops thought I was not doing enough to make Seuthes pay them.

We moved north along the coast and came to

Salmydessus, where a shoal runs far out into the Black Sea. This is a deadly trap for ships; and scattered about the beach we found innumerable cases, mattresses and piles of books, and all the things which sailors carry in their sea chests. This wreckage was so valuable to the Thracians that they had set up pillars on the beach to mark the rights of various owners. It was said that before the boundaries were marked the beachcombers used to fight for the spoil and kill each other.

When all this country had been subjected to Seuthes, we marched south again and took up quarters about three miles from the Sea of Marmara. Here we heard the latest news: that Sparta had changed its foreign policy and declared war on the Persians, and that the Spartan general, Thibron, was about to open a campaign against Tissaphernes.

Thibron sent up two of his officers, Charminus and Polynicus, to try to get hold of our army. And Seuthes, who now had enough native troops of his own, agreed at a secret meeting to hand it over.

I was carefully kept out of the negotiations, for Heracleides knew very well that I should insist on the army's pay, which was the best part of two months behind, being brought up to date. He told the Spartan officers that I was certain to be difficult and advised them to put their proposal direct to the troops.

Heracleides, Charminus, and Polynicus called a soldiers' meeting at which I was bitterly attacked. It was just assumed that I wanted to keep the army in Seuthes' service instead of joining Thibron. And in the eyes of the troops the only possible motive for that was that I must be making money. One of the Arcadians even said that Seuthes had made me rich instead of them, and that he would gladly give up all claim to his pay, if he could watch me stoned to death.

My life depended on what I could say in my own defense. I reminded the army of all their difficulties since they had been flung out of Byzantium, and how I had turned back to help them when I was already on my way home. If they thought that I had received their pay from

Seuthes and not handed it out, then they should force Seuthes to recover it from me.

This was effective, for Seuthes was standing there listening with an interpreter at his side—not that he needed one, for he could understand most of what was said in Greek.

"I haven't been paid any more than you," I went on. "And you may say, if you like, that I was a fool to persuade you into this adventure. But was I? Remember what a state you were in, and what a comfortable winter you have had! You have lost no killed or prisoners. You have been living on the fat of the land. And you have preserved your reputation as an invincible army.

"So much for you. And now look at my side. When I started home, I was—thanks to you—famous through all Greece. And here I am dishonored and distrusted by you, by Seuthes and by these Spartans."

Charminus at once got up and told the army bluntly that they were wrong.

"I myself can be a witness for Xenophon," he

said. "When Polynicus and I asked Seuthes what sort of man he was, Seuthes answered that he had no fault at all to find in him except that he was too much the soldiers' friend, and that this was the only reason why he was in continual trouble with the Prince and with us Spartans."

"All right, then," another of the Arcadians retorted. "If you're going to take command of us, let's see if you can be the soldiers' friend, too. Go and get our pay!"

"Heracleides has got it," shouted Polycrates, my fellow-Athenian. I must admit I put him up to it.

Seuthes and Heracleides didn't stop to hear any more. They mounted their horses and galloped out of reach of the army and didn't stop till they reached their own camp.

After this the Greek and the Thracian camps were at a good, safe distance from one another. But Seuthes and I were never on bad terms. He even wanted me to remain in Thrace with 1,000 infantry of the line, promising us land to colonize and a fortress on the coast.

So, at a last interview, I managed to succeed

where the Spartans had failed. I shamed Seuthes into putting up some pay, pointing out that he was as great a man now as I could make him, and that all he had done for me was to ruin my influence over the army.

He cursed Heracleides for making trouble and never providing any ready cash; then he delivered to me 600 oxen, 4,000 sheep and 120 slaves. I handed the lot over to Charminus and Polynicus and made them do the distribution. By the time they had finished it, they had a clearer idea of how difficult the army could be when pay was in arrears.

I had been away with Seuthes for some weeks, and a rumor had gone around the army that I intended to desert it and stay in Thrace. When I came back, I was welcomed enthusiastically and all was forgotten. And so, after all, it was I who had to take command and hand over the army to Thibron.

We crossed the Dardanelles and landed at Lampsacus. Here I met Eucleides, who was an old friend of my family. His father was the painter who did the walls of the Lyceum, and he himself became a priest—and a very wise one. In the course of our conversation he remarked that he supposed I was now a very rich man. I had to confess that I couldn't pay my passage home until I had sold my horse.

"Have you tried sacrificing to Zeus the Gentle," he asked, "as I used to do for you all at home?"

I never had. Many a time had I prayed and sacrificed to Zeus the King and Zeus the Savior, but not to Zeus the Gentle.

Eucleides said that he was sure my luck would change if I followed the old custom. So I obtained some little pigs and sacrificed them and prayed. The signs were most favorable.

The very next day two of Thibron's staff officers arrived with pay for the army. And as a present for me they brought back my horse, which I had sold for fifty gold pieces in Lampsacus, saying that they knew I was fond of it. This was a most delicate compliment and equivalent to giving me a whole year's pay although they knew I was about to leave the army.

We then marched to join Thibron, past Troy

Xenophon sacrificed and prayed to the god Zeus.

and along the coast of Mysia until we came to
Pergamus. Here was the estate of Gongylus, a
Greek whose family had been banished from
Eretria eighty years earlier for taking the Persian
side in the war with Xerxes. His wife, Hellas,
entertained me with great hospitality.

Hellas told me that Asidates, an enormously
wealthy Persian noble, was staying at his castle
in the valley of the river Caicus with all his family and possessions.

"If you lead out three hundred men," she

said, "and surprise him at night, you'll capture the whole lot of them."

After dinner I set off, taking with me just the officers who had been my closest friends during the long march, as I wanted to do them a good turn. Plenty of others wished to join us, but we would not let them—assuming too readily that we had only to break in and grab Asidates and the loot.

We arrived at midnight. All around the castle were the slaves and the cattle, but we didn't waste time on them. What we wanted was inside.

The castle, however, was much more formidable than we expected. It had a wall eight bricks thick and battlements defended by a garrison which knew its business. Our assault failed, so we started to drive a trench under the walls. By daylight our tunnel was through. But as soon as the leading man knocked out a brick, thereby letting the light in, a great spit used for roasting oxen was plunged into the hole and caught him through the thigh.

The garrison archers kept the tunnel under so

fierce a fire that we could not use it. Meanwhile, the signal beacons were flaming away on the battlements and soon all the available forces of the province were about our ears: cavalry, Assyrian infantry, 800 light troops, and more coming up over the plain from Parthenium and Apollonia.

We cleared out as fast as we could, marching in hollow square and taking with us, in the center of it, all the slaves and cattle we could capture. I can't say we wanted them. We really took them to give ourselves a motive for not running away.

Hellas' son, in spite of his mother's entreaties, came out to the rescue with his personal retainers. So did another of the local Greek exiles with his men. We reached home in safety with 200 prisoners and a flock of sheep, but half of us had been wounded by sling-stones or arrows. Among the casualties was my old friend Agasias, who of course had been fighting and enjoying it from beginning to end.

The next night I led out the whole army as if I intended to resume the march south. I reckoned that we could make another dash for

Asidates' castle when he, thinking we had gone, had relaxed his precautions. But his nerves had broken. He abandoned his castle and tried to escape, and his whole caravan walked right into our army. That's what happens when you make proper sacrifices. We took him for ransom, with his wife and children and all his horses, cattle and treasure.

The army was delighted and decided—Spartans, generals, captains, soldiers and all—to give me a farewell presentation by letting me have first pick at the loot.

Soon afterward I handed over the army to Thibron to be merged with his own, and I returned to Athens.

Index